POEMS

Poetry by

PADRAIC COLUM

DRAMATIC LEGENDS AND OTHER POEMS

WILD EARTH AND OTHER POEMS

OLD PASTURES

CREATURES

PADRAIC COLUM

POEMS

NEW YORK
THE MACMILLAN COMPANY
1932

CONTENTS

REMINISCENCE, DRAMATIC LEGENDS, DRAMATIC IDYLLS

PAGE

Dedication: to M.C.M.C. 3
Reminiscence 4
Queen Gormlai 16
Gilderoy 18
The Miracle of the Corn 19
Swift's Pastoral 38
The Bird of Jesus 44
The Burial of Saint Brendan 47
The Ballad of Downal Baun 50
Polonius and the Ballad Singers 56
Old Men Complaining 60
Girls Spinning 63
Blades 68
Scanderbeg 71
Minoan 73
Indian 74
Hawaiian 75

WILD EARTH

The Plougher 79
The Furrow and the Hearth 81
A Drover 84
A Connachtman 86
A Man Bereaved 88
An Old Woman of the Roads 90
Interior 91

What the Shuiler Said as She Lay by the Fire in the
  Farmer's House 92
Spinning Songs 94
The Knitters 98
Folding Hour 99
The Terrible Robber Men 100
Garadh 101
A Rann of Exile 102
Old Soldier 103
The Tin-Whistle Player 104
A Mountaineer 105
Sojourning and Wandering 106
Shall I Go Bound and You Go Free? 108
She Moved Through the Fair 109
Across the Door 110
A Cradle Song 111
The Sister's Lullaby 112
The Beggar's Child 113
No Child 114
An Drinaun Donn 115
The Poor Girl's Meditation 117
Dermott Donn Macmorna 119
A Poor Scholar of the 'Forties 120
A Saint 121
The Toy-Maker 123
A Ballad Maker 125
The Poet 127

OTHER LANDS AND SEAS

Arab Songs 131
"I Shall Not Die for Thee" 134

An Idyll 135

Legend 136

Men on Islands 137

Branding the Foals 138

Imitation of a Welsh Poem 139

To a Poet 140

First East to West Atlantic Flyers 141

The Wayfarer 142

In the Carolina Woods 144

Hawaii 145

CREATURES

David Ap Gwillan at the Mass of the Birds 153

Jackdaw 154

Crows 156

Otters 157

Asses 158

Pigeons 162

Swallow 165

Crane 166

The Little Fox 167

Wild Ass 168

Monkeys 169

Bison 171

Snake 172

Aquarium Fish 173

Night-Fliers 174

Bat 175

Bird of Paradise 176

Humming-Bird 177

The Resplendent Quetzal-Bird 178

	PAGE
VULTURES	179
HORNETS	180
PLOVERS	181
CONDORS	182

OLD PASTURES

DUBLIN ROADS	185
LABURNUMS	188
LILAC BLOSSOMS	189
FUCHSIA HEDGES IN CONNACHT	190
AT CASHAL	191
THE OLD COLLEGE OF THE IRISH, PARIS	192
SONG OF STARLINGS	193
VERSES FOR ALFEO FAGGI'S STATIONS OF THE CROSS	194
BREFFNE CAOINE	200
ON TWO SISTERS WHOSE DEATHS WERE TOGETHER	201
IN MEMORY OF JOHN BUTLER YEATS	202
THE RUNE-MASTER	203
ODYSSEUS: IN MEMORY OF ARTHUR GRIFFITH	205
ROGER CASEMENT	207
BEFORE THE FAIR	208
AVE ATQUE VALE	209
THE LANDING	210

NOTES	213
INDEX TO FIRST LINES	217
INDEX TO TITLES	219

REMINISCENCE, DRAMATIC LEGENDS,
DRAMATIC IDYLLS

Dedication: *to M. C. M. C.*

THE well—
They come to it and take
Their cupful or their palmful out of it.

The well—
Stones are around it, and an elder bush
Is there; a high rowan tree; and so
The well is marked.

Who knows
Whence come the waters? Through what passages
Beneath? From what high tors
Where forests are? Forests dripping rain!
Branches pouring to the ground; trunks, barks, roots,
Letting the streamlets down: through the dark earth
The water flows, and in that secret flood
That's called a spring, that finds this little hollow.
Who knows
Whence come the waters that fill cup and palm?

Sweetheart and comrade, I give you
The waters' marches and the forest's bound,
The valley-filling cloud, the trees that set
The rains beneath their roots, out of this well.

Reminiscence

I

The Swallows sang
ALIEN to us are
   Your fields, and your cotes, and your glebes;
Secret our nests are
   Although they be built in your eaves;
Un-eaten by us are
   The grains that grow in your fields.

The Weathercock on the barn answered
Not alien to ye are
   The powers of un-earthbound beings:
Their curse ye would bring
   On our cotes, and our glebes, and our fields,
If aught should befall
   The brood that is bred in the eaves.

The Swallows answered
If aught should befall
   Our brood that's not travelled the seas,
Your temples would fall,
   And blood ye would milk from your beeves:
Against them the curse we would bring
   Of un-earthbound beings!

II

I saw the wind to-day:
I saw it in the pane
Of glass upon the wall:

4

A moving thing—'twas like
No bird with widening wing,
No mouse that runs along
The meal bag under the beam.

I think it like a horse,
All black, with frightening mane,
That springs out of the earth,
And tramples on his way.
I saw it in the glass,
The shaking of a mane:
A horse that no one rides!

III

Jews' harps and masks and kites,
And paper-lanterns with their farthen-lights,
All in a dim-lit window to be seen:
Within—
The walls that have the patches of the damp,
The counter where there burns the murky lamp,
And then, the counter and the shelf between,
The dame,
Meagre, grey-polled, lame.

Meet for a town where pennies have few pairs
In children's pockets, this toy-shop with its wares:
And here she's been since times are legendary;
For Miler Dowdall, whom we used to see
Upon the hoardings with deft hands held up
To win the champion's belt or silver cup,
Would come in here to buy a ball or top—
That Miler Dowdall the great pugilist

5

Who had the world once beneath his fist,
Whose name is now a name that's blown by!

How's custom? Bad enough; she had not sold
Six kites this present year for boys to hold—
She sold them by the gross in times agone;
Marbles, none.
Wasn't it poor, the town
Where boys
Could not buy marbles, leaving other calls—
Where little girls could hardly pay for dolls?

But she's not tragical—no, not a bit:
She laughs as she talks to you—that is it!
Her eyes are bright,
As in paper-lanterns farthen-candles' light,
And like a kite
Her lame, spare frame's upborne—
A paper kite held by a string that's worn;
And like a Jew's harp when you strike its tongue—
Her voice goes on!

And she will hop
The inches of her crib, this narrow shop,
When you step in to be her customer:
A bird of little worth, a sparrow, say,
Whose crib's in some neglected passage-way,
And one's left wondering who brings crumbs to her.
How strange to think that she is still inside
After so many turns of the tide—
Since this lit window was a dragon's eye
To turn us all to wonder coming nigh—
Since this dim window was a dragon's eye!

IV

Down a street that once I lived in
You used to pass, a honey-seller,
And the town in which that street was
Was the shabbiest of all places;
You were different from the others
Who went by to barter meanly:
Different from the man with colored
Windmills for the children's pennies;
Different from the drab purveyor
With her paper screens to fill up
Chill and empty fireplaces.

You went by, a man upstanding,
On your head a wide dish, holding
Dark and golden lumps of honey;
You went slowly, like an old horse
That's not driven any longer,
But that likes to take an amble.

No one ever bought your honey,
No one ever paid a penny
For a single comb of sweetness;
Every house was grim unto you
With foregone desire of eating
Bread whose taste had sweet of honey.

Yet you went, a man contented
's though you had a king to call on
Who would take you to his parlour,
And buy all your stock of honey.
On you went, and in a sounding

7

Voice, just like the bell of evening,
Told us of the goods you carried,
Told us of the dark and golden
Treasure dripping on your wide dish.

You went by, and no one named you!

V

The crows still fly to that wood, and out of the wood she
comes,
Carrying her load of sticks, a little less now than before,
Her strength being less; she bends as the hoar rush bends in
the wind;
She will sit by the fire, in the smoke, her thoughts on root and
the living branch no more.

The crows still fly to that wood, that wood that is sparse and
gapped;
The last one left of the herd makes way by the lane to the stall,
Lowing distress as she goes; the great trees there are all down;
No fiddle sounds in the hut to-night, and a candle only gives
light to the hall.

The trees are gapped and sparse, yet a sapling spreads on the
joints
Of the wall, till the castle stones fall down into the moat:
The last one who minds that our race once stood as a spreading
tree,
She goes, and thorns are bare, where the blackbird, his summer
songs done, strikes one metal note.

8

VI

The Mountain Thrush I say,
But I am thinking of her, Nell the Rambler:
She'd come down to our houses bird-alone,
From some haunt that was hers, and we would see her
Drawing the water from the well one day,
For one house or another, or we'd hear her
Garrulous with the turkeys down the street,
We children.

From neighbour's house to neighbour's house she'd go
Until one day we'd see
Her worn cloak hanging behind our door;
And then, that night, we'd hear
Of Earl Gerald: how he rides abroad,
His horse's hooves shod with the weighty silver,
And how he'll ride all roads till those silver shoes
Are worn thin;
As thin as the cat's ears before the fire,
Upraised in such content before the fire,
And making little lanterns in the firelight.

The Mountain Thrush, when every way's a hard one,
Hops on in numbness till a patch of sunlight,
Falling, will turn her to a wayside song;
So it was with her, Rambler Nell, a shelter,
A bit upon the board, and she flowed on
With rambler's discourse—tales, and rhymes, and sayings,
With child's light in her worn eyes, and laughter
To all her words.

The lore she had—
'Twas like a kingly robe, on which long rains

9

Have fallen and fallen, and parted
The finely woven web, and have washed away
The kingly colours, but have left some threads
Still golden, and some feathers still as shining
As the kingfisher's. While she sat there, not spinning,
Not weaving anything but her own fancies,
We ate potatoes out of the ash, and thought them
Like golden apples out of Tiprobane.

When winter's over-long, and days that famish
Come one upon another like snowflakes,
The Mountain Thrush makes way down to our houses:
Hops round for crumbs, and stays a while, a comer
Upon our floors.

She did not think
Bread of dependence bitter; three went with her—
Hunger, Sorrow, and Loneliness—and they
Had crushed all that makes claims, though they'd not bent her,
Nor emptied her of trust—what was it led her
From house to house, but that she always looked for
A warmer welcome at the hearth ahead?

So she went on until it came one day
The Mountain Thrush's heart-stop on the way.

VII

An old man said, "I saw
The chief of the things that are gone;
A stag with head held high,
A doe, and a fawn;

"And they were the deer of Ireland
That scorned to breed within bound:
The last; they left no race
Tame on a pleasure-ground.

"A stag, with his hide all rough
With the dew, and a doe and a fawn;
Nearby, on their track on the mountain,
I watched them, two and one,

"Down to the Shannon going—
Did its waters cease to flow
When they passed, they that carried the swiftness
And the pride of long ago?

"The last of the troop that had heard
Finn's and Oscar's cry;
A doe and a fawn, and before,
A stag with head held high!"

VIII

"A Stranger you came to me over the Sea,
But welcome I made you, Seumas-a-ree,
And shelter I gave you, my sons set to ward you,
Red war I faced for you, Seumas-a-ree.

"Now a craven you go from me over the Sea,
But my best sons go with you, Seumas-a-ree;
Foreign graves they will gain, and for those who remain
The black hemp is sown—och, Seumas-a-ree!

"But the Boyne shall flow back from the wide Irish Sea,
On the Causeway of Aughrim our victory shall be:

Two hundreds of years and the child on the knee
Will be rocked to this cronach, Seumas-a-ree!"

IX

You blew in
Where Jillin Brady kept up state on nothing,
Married her daughter, and brought to Jillin's house
A leash of dogs, a run of ferrets, a kite
In a wired box; linnets and larks and gold-finches
In their proper cages; and you brought with you this song:

> If you come to look for me,
> Perhaps you'll not me find:
> For I'll not in my Castle be—
> Inquire where horns wind.

> Before I had a man-at-arms
> I had an eager hound:
> Then was I known as Reynardine,
> In no crib to be found.

You used to say
Five hounds' lives were a man's life, and when Teague
Had died of old age, and when Fury that was a pup
When Teague was maundering, had turned from hill to hearth
And lay in the dimness of a hound's old age,
I went with you again, and you were upright
As the circus-rider standing on his horse;
Quick as a goat that will take any path, and lean—
Lean as a lash; you'd have no speech
With wife or child or mother-in-law till you
Were out of doors and standing on the ditch
Ready to face the river or the hill:

Then Hen-wife's son once heard the grouse
Talk to his soft-voiced mate;
And what he heard the health-poult say
The loon would not relate.

Impatient in the yard he grew,
And patient on the hill;
Of cocks and hens he'd take no charge,
And he went with Reynardine.

Lean days when we were idle as the birds,
That will not preen their feathers, but will travel
To taste a berry, or pull a shred of wool
That they will never use. We pass the bounds:
A forest's grave, the black bog is before us,
And in its very middle you will show me
The snipe's nest that is lonelier than the snipe
That's all that's there; and then a stony hill,
A red fox climbing, pausing, looking round his tail
At us travailing against wind and rain
To reach the river-spring where Finn or Fergus
Hardened a spear, back of a thousand years.

And still your cronies are what they were then—
The hounds that know the hill and know the hearth
(One is Fury that's as old as Argos now
That crawled to Odysseus coming back);
Your minstrels, the blackbird singing still
When kites are leaving, crows are going home,
And the thrush in the morning like a spectre showing
Beside the day-spring; and your visitors,
The cuckoo that will swing upon a branch,
The corncrake with quick head between the grass-tufts.

And still your song is what it used to be—
About that Reynardine who came to lord
A castle (O that castle with its trees!),
Who heard the horns, and let his turret grow
The foxglove where his banner should be seen:

> The hawk is for the hill, he cried,
> The badger for the glen;
> The otter for the river-pools—
> Amen, amen, amen!

X

At the fore of the year, and on Candlemas Day,
All early at Mass I remarked her—
Like the dew on green corn, as bright and as clear
Were her eyes, and her voice was the starling's!

With bragging and lies, I thought that her mind
I'd engage, and then win her with praises,
But through Spring and through Summer she has left me to rise
Every day with a pain that will slay me!

Oh, come, O my love, ere the life from me goes
If your hand but to lightly lay on me,
And a grief take away that none else can remove—
For now 'tis the reaping of barley!

XI

It would not be far for us two to go back to the age of bronze:
Then you were a king's daughter, your father had curraghs on
        hore,
A herd of horses, good tillage upon the face of four hills,

And clumps of cattle beyond them where rough-browed men
    showed their spears.

And I was good at the bow, but had no men, no herds,
And your father would have bestowed you in a while on some
    unrenowned
Ulysses, or on the old king to whom they afterwards raised
Three stones as high as the elk's head (this cromlech, maybe,
    where we sit)

How fair you were when you walked beside the old forest trees!
So fair that I thought you would change and fly away as a swan,
And then we were mates for play, and then all eagle you grew
To drive me to range the tempest—king's child of the hero-age!

I called three times as an owl: through the gap where the herds-
    men watched
You ran, and we climbed the height where the brackens pushed
    at our knees;
And we lay where the brackens drew the earth-smell out of the
    earth,
And we journeyed and baffled the fighters of three ill-wishing
    kings!

It would not be far for us two to go back to the age of bronze—
The fire left by the nomads is lone as a burning ship!
We eat them as we pass by, the ears of the sweet green wheat!
At last, a king, I relieve a good clan from a dragon's spleen!

Pieces of amber I brought you, big as a bowman's thumbs,
Trumpets I left beside you, wrought when the smiths had all art,
A dancing-bird that I caught you—they are back in the age of
    bronze:
I give what I made, and found, and caught—a score of songs!

Queen Gormlai

Nor fingers that e'er felt
Fine things within their hold
Drew needles in and through,
And smoothed out the fold,
And put the hodden patch
Upon the patch of grey—
Unseemly is the garb
That's for my back to-day!

O skinflint woman, Mór,
Who knows that I speak true—
I had women once,
A queen's retinue;
And they were ones who knew
The raiment of a queen;
Their thoughts were on my tire,
Their minds were on my mien!

Light of hand and apt,
And companionable,
Seven score women, Mór,
I had at my call,
Who am to-day begrudged
The blink of candle-light
To put it on, the garb,
That leaves me misbedight.

I wore a blue Norse hood
The time I watched the turns
And feats of Clann O'Neill—
We quaffed from goblet-horns;

A crimson cloak I wore
When, with Niall the King,
I watched the horses race
At Limerick in the Spring!

In Tara of King Niall
The gold was round the wine,
And I was given the cup—
A furze-bright dress was mine;
And now this clout to wear
Where I rise to sup whey,
With root-like stitches through
The hodden on the grey!

No more upon the board
Candles for kings are lit,
No more can I bid her
And her bring gowning fit;
The bramble is no friend—
It pulls at me and drags;
The thorny ground is mine
Where briars tear my rags!

Gilderoy

THE smith who made the manacles,
With bar and bolt, and link and ring,
Sang out above his hearty blows—
"I can't have grief for everything."

As Roger by the rope-walk went
The bramble-bird cheeped up to sing;
He cut the wanted coil, and said—
"I can't have grief for everything."

The lad who came to Ladder Lane,
And saw his hemp-cravat a-string,
"Jack's doom 's Jill's dule," he said, "but then,
I can't have grief for everything."

And I who carried bag and wig,
Looked up and saw him turn and swing;
The dog he gave fixed eyes on me—
Can I have grief for everything?

The Miracle of the Corn

People in the Legend

FARDORROUGHA	*A Farmer*
PAUDEEN	*Fardorrougha's Servant:*
	a Fool
SHEILA	*Fardorrougha's Wife*
AISLINN	*A Child*
THREE WOMEN	
SHAUN O' THE BOG	*A Poor Man*

The action passes in a farmer's house in the old times.

SCENE: *The interior of* FARDORROUGHA's *house. The door at back R.; the hearth L.; the window R. is only conventionally represented. What is actually shown is a bin for corn (corn in the sense of any kind of grain, as the word is used in Ireland—the breadstuff and the symbol of fertility), shelves with vessels, benches, and a shrine. The bin projects from back C.; the shelves with vessels are each side of the bin; the shrine is R.; it holds a small statue of the Blessed Virgin, and a rosary of large beads hangs from it; the benches are R. and L. One is at the conventional fireplace, and the other is down from the conventional door.*

All the persons concerned in the action are on the scene when it opens, and they remain on the scene. They only enter the action when they go up to where the bin is. Going back to the places they had on the benches takes them out of the action.

On the bench near the hearth sit the people of FARDORROUGHA's *household—*FARDORROUGHA, SHEILA, PAUDEEN, AISLINN. *On the bench near the door sit the strangers—three women, one of whom has a child with her, and* SHAUN O' THE BOG. *The people are dressed in greys and browns, and brown is the colour of the*

19

interior. The three women and SHAUN O' THE BOG *are poorly dressed; the women are barefooted.* PAUDEEN *is dressed rudely, and sandals of hide are bound across his feet.* FARDORROUGHA, SHEILA, *and* AISLINN *are comfortably dressed.*

PAUDEEN

They're moaning still,
The cattle. Will they never stop
Their moaning, Master Fardorrougha?

FARDORROUGHA

We could drive the cattle
To another place, but the house would not be safe
While we were gone; we know well, Paudeen,
There are those who would break in my door.

PAUDEEN

Aye, the people
Are bad from want. The people have to watch
The black rain and it falling all the day.

FARDORROUGHA

We've hay enough
For our own cows. Give them a lock
Of what the widow of Seumas saved.

PAUDEEN

Is it that
That's under the hurdles behind the hedge?

FARDORROUGHA

Aye. She puts lean beasts upon me, and she owes me
Their fattening.

PAUDEEN

I'll do your bidding, Master.

(PAUDEEN *goes back to his place on the bench.* AISLINN *comes to the bin.*)

FARDORROUGHA

What child is this?

AISLINN

Aislinn is my name.

FARDORROUGHA

Who was it
Gave you that name? It is strange to name
Anyone in the world Aislinn: Dream.

AISLINN

My own people
Gave me that name. And now you'll wonder
What brings me to your house. Sheila, your wife,
Has brought me here to keep her company.

FARDORROUGHA

And you are welcome. There are no young ones here.

AISLINN

I am well used
To doing things about a house, and I
Can sweep the floor, and make a fire, too,
And mind the children.

FARDORROUGHA

There are no children in the house you've come to.
Are you not, child, afeard of me?

AISLINN

No, Fardorrougha, I am not afeard.

FARDORROUGHA

You are like
The brown bird in the cage.

AISLINN

What has Sheila
Upon her altar? I would like to see:
It is the image of the Mother of God!
O why will the rain,
Mother of God, keep falling? It destroyed
The harvest! Why will the black rain keep falling now?

(FARDORROUGHA *goes back to the bench.* SHEILA *goes to* AISLINN.)

SHEILA

It is the will of God.

AISLINN

God's will is set
Against us all; it is set against
The cattle in the field, and it was they
Stood by His crib; they're moaning always now:
He has forgotten them.

SHEILA

Do not be listening to
The cattle moaning; do not be watching
The black rain and it falling all the day.

AISLINN

You He has not forgotten.

SHEILA

God has not forgotten me, Aislinn.

AISLINN

If He left
Your fields to the rain, He knows that you
Have a good roof and plenty under it.

SHEILA

To have them is no sign
That God remembers one: I used to look
Upon my roof and riches, and yet say,
"You have forgotten me, Almighty God!"

AISLINN

And could you say that
When there was corn: "You have forgotten me!"?

SHEILA

When I would look
Upon my fields and they heavy with the crop,
"You have remembered the furrows," I would say,
"And they are fruitful, but you have forgotten
The woman Sheila!"
And now when the furrows are forgotten He
Remembers me. O Aislinn, child,
Your arms around me—I would have you near:
I want
Your face before me; I would have a face
Like yours, but glad; a child's face glad and bright!

(PAUDEEN *goes to the bin and opens it.*)

PAUDEEN

It's empty, and it will take some filling.
It's empty, and you could put more than a capful in it.
It's empty, and it will hold an apronful.

SHEILA

What are you doing at the bin, Paudeen?

PAUDEEN

Making it ready to put corn in it.
"Better have the corn in the bin," said he,
"Than in the barn, after what happened
In the barn," said he.

SHEILA ___

What was it happened?

PAUDEEN

"And only Gorav, my good dog," said he,
"Got the man by the throat,
There would be a thief in the parish, and a poor man," said he.

SHEILA

The hard, hard man!

PAUDEEN

"There's a good door to my house," said he,
"And a bin's within, and if the priest," said he,
"Can't put the fear of God into the people,
Gorav, maybe, can," said he.

That's empty—there's not a grain inside it.

(PAUDEEN *goes back to his place on the bench.*)

SHEILA

He has all
The corn that's in the country, and he sets
Gorav to guard it. The people bring their cattle
Before he gives them corn to keep them living.

AISLINN

I'm not afeard
Of Fardorrougha.

SHEILA

He is not set
In hardness yet; he will give back in armfuls
What he took in his hands.

AISLINN

Will it be long till then?

SHEILA

Not long, not long;
The fruit is ripening that will bring him to
Himself. Oh, Aislinn, do not think
Too hardly of my man; there was no child
About our house, Aislinn!

(FARDORROUGHA *goes to the bin, bringing with him a sack of corn.*)

FARDORROUGHA

Woman of the house, be careful that you put
The big bolt on the door when it gets dark.

SHEILA

Let it not come
Between you and your rest, Fardorrougha.

FARDORROUGHA

I grudge
To give them corn even for what they bring.

SHEILA

Look at Aislinn:
Would you not let it all go with the wind
To have a child like Aislinn?

FARDORROUGHA

Woman, content yourself
With what is given.

SHEILA

God has given us
House and mill, land and riches, but not
Content.

FARDORROUGHA

Then let what is not
Trouble us not.

SHEILA

Aislinn was with me all the day; Aislinn
Will fill the bin for you. Aislinn, take
A measure off the dresser, and help Fardorrougha
Empty the sack.

26

FARDORROUGHA

It was a woman, surely,
That named her Aislinn: Dream.

SHEILA

She is a biddable child, and one that's good
About a house.

FARDORROUGHA

She'll have no need
To do much while she's here.

SHEILA

Isn't it well, Fardorrougha,
To see a child that isn't white-faced?

FARDORROUGHA

The corn into the bin!

SHEILA

Isn't it a comfort
To see a child like Aislinn here? Then think
Of a glad, bright child!

FARDORROUGHA

I have no thought
To go that far. That world,
The world of bud and blossom, has gone by;
There's only now,
The ragged sky, the poor and wasted ground . . .

SHEILA

No, Fardorrougha, no!
Listen to me, Fardorrougha!

27

FARDORROUGHA
. . . And broken beings like Paudeen!

SHEILA
No, Fardorrougha.

FARDORROUGHA
Well, my woman.

SHEILA
I have something,
Fardorrougha, to tell you.

FARDORROUGHA
And I am listening, woman.

(PAUDEEN *goes to the bin.*)

PAUDEEN
Shaun o' the Bog is on the pass
Before the barn.

FARDORROUGHA
Before the barn? Is it me he wants?

PAUDEEN
It's for the woman
Of the house he's asking. "Is she by herself?"
Says he to me.

FARDORROUGHA
She's not by herself
If that's the chance he's seeking. You, Sheila,

Had something else you would have said to me:
"Loose the corn you have gathered," maybe.
Never say it,
Or the harsh word that has not been, will be
Between us.

I'll see the man, and if he wants to make
A bargain that is fair, it's with myself
That he must make it.

(FARDORROUGHA *goes back to the bench.* PAUDEEN *has some hay in his hands. He has taken it from under where he sat.*)

PAUDEEN
Where did he say
I was to put the hay that was under the hedge?

SHEILA
Where the cows are. Oh,
How can your mind keep on the hay? I know:
It's because you are simple! Aye . . .
Paudeen,
Why do they call you fool? Why
Do they think he's foolish, Aislinn?

AISLINN
It is because
His mind keeps on the one thing only.

SHEILA
He can see
Only the hay that's in his hands. But then
They're all foolish! Paudeen, I tell you

They who gathered thoughts while in the womb
Are foolish now as you are.

PAUDEEN

(*drawing his foot across the floor*) But you said
I was a clean and well-built boy, anyhow,
Woman of the house.

SHEILA

Yes, I said it.

(PAUDEEN *goes back to the bench*.)

AISLINN

I'm not afeard
Of Fardorrougha: I do not think him hard.

SHEILA

His heart opened to you, and that's a sign—
Yes, that's a sign I take.

AISLINN

And do you think that he would ever give
The harsh word to you?

SHEILA

O Aislinn, pray:
Pray that it will never come to that; the thought
Of the harsh word from him has come to me
Again and again, like some dark bird.

AISLINN

And have you never had
The harsh word from your man?

SHEILA

But now
The harsh word would be the end of all.
Listen to me:
Outside the rain
Is falling, and its desolation
Is all around me. If he gave me
The harsh word, the desolation
Would fill me, then what fruit could be?
O glad, bright, shining, tender
Apple-blossom, what fruit would you make
And the tree of you under desolation?

(*The* THREE WOMEN *leave the bench and come to the bin. One
has a child with her.*)

SHEILA

What can I do for you, women?

FIRST WOMAN

We have eaten
Nettles and roots since the want came, we
And our children.

SECOND WOMAN

Our children droop. You do not know what it is
To see a child droop.

THIRD WOMAN

God has not opened
Doors of madness and pain for you.

(SHEILA *takes a vessel and holds it to a child who drinks.*)

31

FIRST WOMAN
Do not forget my child.

SHEILA
Take
What is in my house, women.

(*She opens the bin and fills a woman's apron with corn. The other women hold out their aprons.* SHEILA *fills them.*)

FIRST WOMAN
May God
Heap up store for you, and may you
Have clan with store.

SECOND WOMAN
May God be with your husband when his hand
Scatters the seed, and may his labour be
Prosperous!

THIRD WOMAN
And may your own labour be
Light, and watched by the Mother of God!

SHEILA
Women, who am I
That you should pray for me!

(*The women go to the bench.* SHEILA *stands quiet.* AISLINN *goes to her.*)

AISLINN
Now there is no more
Of Fardorrougha's corn.

SHEILA

But God will have love
And pity for us.

AISLINN

The bin is emptied. Will Fardorrougha . . .

SHEILA

Oh, hush!
There is the cattles' moan; here is Paudeen
Who brings them hay—Paudeen who is
With broken things! My heart is heavy again!

AISLINN

Fardorrougha. . . .

SHEILA

Fardorrougha! I had forgotten him.
Protect me, God!

The rain, the rain! The black and ragged sky,
The poor and wasted ground—how could there be
Any but Paudeen's like?

PAUDEEN

(*going to bin*) But you said,
Yourself, I was a clean and well-built boy.

SHEILA

I said it. And now, Paudeen,
Open the bin.

(PAUDEEN *opens the front of the bin; it is shown to be empty.*)

13238   33

PAUDEEN

Oh, what will we tell
Fardorrougha? Can any of you think
Of a story to tell him?

SHEILA

We can tell him
No story at all.

AISLINN

But we might
Keep him from opening of the bin.

SHEILA

No, Aislinn, no:
No good would be in that.

It was the right I did. Their children now
Crowd round them. O children, I would give
Bread to you again, and over again!

I, too,
Was one of them who had their minds upon
One thing only; I hardened, too,
To make things easy for myself. It is not
"God protect me," I should be saying now,
But "God forgive me!"

(SHAUN O' THE BOG *comes from the bench. He goes to the bin.*)

SHAUN

Fardorrougha told me
To wait upon him here.

SHEILA

And what has Fardorrougha
Promised you, Shaun?

SHAUN

The corn in the bin. And I have given
My wool and loom for it.

SHEILA

He has not what he thinks he has, but you
Will not go empty because of that.

SHAUN

It is well for Aislinn
To be with you in this house.

SHEILA

Aislinn, go talk to Shaun; he need not be
Anxious nor fretted.

AISLINN

Nor need you be
Anxious nor fretted, Sheila.

SHEILA

I am not anxious any more, Aislinn.

(FARDORROUGHA *goes to the bin.*)

FARDORROUGHA

The corn is here that I will give you, Shaun,
For wool and loom; open, you, the bin,
And see what's in it.

(SHAUN *opens front of bin. A very great quantity of corn gushes out.*)

FARDORROUGHA

I did not think
So much was there. He'll not get all
For wool and loom; I will not wrong myself;
As much as half is fair.

(*He turns to the bin and sees that* SHAUN, SHEILA, *and* AISLINN *are kneeling beside the heap of corn.*)

FARDORROUGHA

Why are you kneeling, Shaun?

SHAUN

I kneel because I know
My children will be fed.

FARDORROUGHA

Why are you kneeling, Sheila?

SHEILA

I kneel because I know
The fields will break to corn because of the love
And pity God has for us.

FARDORROUGHA

Why are you kneeling, Aislinn?

AISLINN

I kneel because I know
A miracle has happened; Sheila need not dread
The harsh word from you any more nor never.

An air comes from it all—a smell of growing
Green, growing corn; and I mind that I
Brought Sheila from her mother's to this house
Across a field of corn that smelled sweet, sweet,
And whispered lovingly. I am greatly changed,
And often I am strange even to myself.
What good 's in what I've gathered? It's between
Myself and her; but when she rises now
Nothing will be between us; at what she'll say
All I have gathered I shall give away.

(*With* SHEILA, AISLINN *and* SHAUN *still kneeling, the scene closes.*)

Swift's Pastoral

A story that has for its background Saint Patrick's Purgatory.

Characters:

JONATHAN SWIFT *and* ESTHER VANHOMRIGH

ESTHER

I know the answer: 'tis ingenious.
I'm tired of your riddles, Doctor Swift.

SWIFT

Faith, so am I.

ESTHER

But that's no reason why you'll be splenetic.

SWIFT

Then let us walk.

ESTHER

But will you talk, too? Oh, is there nothing
For you to show your pupil on this highway?

SWIFT

The road to Dublin, and the road that leads
Out of this sunken island.

ESTHER

I see a Harper:
A Harper and a country lout, his fellow,
Upon the highway.

SWIFT

I know the Harper.

ESTHER

The Doctor knows so much, but what of that?
He'll stay splenetic.

SWIFT

I have seen this Harper
On many a road. I know his name, too—
I know a story that they tell about him.

ESTHER

And will it take the pucker off his brow
If Cadenus to Vanessa tell the tale?

SWIFT

God knows it might. His name's O'Carolan—
Turlough O'Carolan; and there is a woman
To make the story almost pastoral.

ESTHER

Some Sheelah or some Oonagh, I'll engage.

SWIFT

Her name
Was Bridget Cruise. She would not wed him,
And he wed one who had another name,
And made himself a Minstrel, but a Minstrel
Of consequence. His playing on the harp
Was the one glory that in Ireland stayed
After lost battles and old pride cast down.
Where he went men would say:

"Horses we may not own, nor swords may carry,
But Turlough O'Carolan plays upon the harp,
And Turlough O'Carolan's ten fingers bring us
Horses and swords, gold, wine, and victory."

ESTHER
Oh, that is eloquence!

SWIFT
I know their rhapsodies. But to O'Carolan:
He played, and drank full cups; made proper songs
In praise of banquets, wine-cups, and young maids—
Things easily praised. And then when he was old—

ESTHER
How old?

SWIFT
Two score of years and ten.

ESTHER
But that's not old.

SWIFT
And that's not old! Good God, how soon we grow
Into the Valley of the Shadow of Death!—
Not into the Valley, Vanessa, mark, of Death,
But into the Shadow! Two score years and ten—
Have we not three score and some more to live?
So has the tree that's withered at the top—
Dead in the head! Aye, we, Vanessa, grow
Into the Shadow, and in the Shadow stay
So long!

ESTHER

I thought the story would divert Cadenus.

SWIFT

It will, it will, Vanessa. What was I
Just saying?

ESTHER

When he was old. . . .

SWIFT

And blind—did I say he was blind?

ESTHER

You did not say it.

SWIFT

He's blind—not book-blind, but stone-blind.
He cannot see
The wen that makes two heads upon the fellow
That goes beside him, hunched up with the harp;
He cannot see
The Justice to the assizes riding
With soldiers all in red to give him state.
He cannot see
The beggar's lice and sores.

I tell a story:
When this O'Carolan was old and blind,
As I have said, he made the pilgrimage:
'Twas to. . . . No, no, 'twas not the place
That I'm proscribed to, but yet one that's called
Saint Patrick's Purgatory.

'Tis on an island in a lake, a low
Island or islet. The water round
Is dun, unsunned; there are no meadows near,
No willows grow, no lark nor linnet sings;
The banks there take a bleakness from the clouds.
A fissure in the island leads down to
The Purgatory of Souls, their fable says.

And now the Harper is but one of those,
The countless wretches, who have brought their sores
To that low island, and brought darkened spirits—
Such stream has flowed there for a thousand years.
I do not know
What length of time the Harper stays, while crowds
Are shambling all around him, weeping, praying,
Famishing themselves, or drinking the dun water
Of the lake for wine; or kneeling, with their knees
On sharpened stones; or crowded
In narrow, stony cells.

ESTHER
It is a place
Papistical.

SWIFT
It is a place
Most universal. De we not walk
Upon a ground that's drenched with tears, and breathe
An air that's thickened with men's darkened spirits?
Aye, and on an islet,
Suffering pain, and hearing cries of wretches:
Cut off, remote, banished, alone, tormented!
Name the place as you will, or let it be
Saint Patrick's Purgatory.

42

But comes a time the blind man rows to shore
From that low island. He touches shore, and cries
"Hands for a blind man's help!" and hands were held him—
He touched a hand.

Here then's the pastoral:
The hand, the fingers of the hand, the clasp
The spirit flowing through—he knew them all;
He knew all well, and in an instant knew them,
And he cried out, "The hand of Bridget Cruise!"

Oh, in the midmost of our darkened spirits
To touch a hand, and know the truth within it—
The truth that's clasped, that holds, the truth that's all
For us—for every day we live, the truth!
To touch that hand, and then once more to turn—
To turn around upon the world's highway,
And go alone—poor hand, poor hand!

But she,
This Bridget Cruise, was leaving that dull shore
For that low island, and had cares beyond
The memory of O'Carolan. Well, they passed,
He going and she coming: well, and then
He took his harp, and the country lout, his fellow,
Went with him, as we see them going now.

ESTHER
They've passed: there's no one now beside us.
And will you take my hand? You used to call me
A white witch, but there is no witchery
In this plain hand of mine!

You've told a double story, Doctor Swift.

43

The Bird of Jesus

It was pure indeed,
The air we breathed in, the light we saw,
I and my brother, when we played that day,
Or piped to one another; then there came
Two young lads of an age with one another,
And with us two, and these two played with us,
And went away.

Each had a bearing that was like a prince's,
Yet they were simple lads and had the kindness
Of our own folk—lads simple and unknowing:
Then, afterwards, we went to visit them.

Theirs was a village that was not far off,
But out of reach—towards elbow, not towards hand:
And what was there were houses—
Houses and some trees—
And it was like a place within a fold.

We found the lads,
And found them still as simple and unknowing,
And played with them: we played outside the stall
Where worked the father of the wiser lad—
Not brothers were the boys, but cousins' children.

There was a pit:
We brought back clay and sat beside the stall,
And made birds out of clay; and then my brother
Took up his bird and flung it in the air:
His playmate did as he,
And clay fell down upon the face of clay.

44

And then I took
The shavings of the board the carpenter
Was working on, and flung them in the air,
And watched them streaming down.

There would be nought to tell
Had not the wiser of the lads took up
The clay he shaped: a little bird it was;
He tossed it from his hand up to his head;
The bird stayed in the air.

O what delight we had
To see it fly and pause, that little bird,
Sinking to earth sometimes, and sometimes rising
As though to fly into the very sun;
At last it spread out wings and flew, and flew,
Flew to the sun.

I do not think
That we played any more, or thought of playing,
For every drop of blood our bodies held
Was free and playing, free and playing then.
Four lads together on the bench we sat:
Nothing was in the open air around us,
And yet we thought something was there for us—
A secret, charmed thing.

So we went homeward; by soft ways we went
That wound us back to our familiar place.
Some increase lay upon the things we saw:
I'll speak of grasses, but you'll never know
What grass was there; words wither it and make it
Like to the desert children's dream of grass;

Lambs in the grass, but I will not have shown you
What fleece of purity they had to show;
I'll speak of birds, but I will not have told you
How their song filled the heart; and when I speak
Of him, my brother, you will never guess
How we two were at one!

Even to our mother we had gained in grace!

The Burial of Saint Brendan

On the third day from this (Saint Brendan said)
I will be where no wind that filled a sail
Has ever been, and it blew high or low:
For from this home-creek, from this body's close
I shall put forth: make ready, you, to go
With what remains to Cluan Hy-many,
For there my resurrection I'd have be.

But you will know how hard they'll strive to hold
This body o' me, and hold it for the place
Where I was bred, they say, and born and reared.
For they would have my resurrection here,
So that my sanctity might be matter shared
By every mother's child the tribeland polled
Who lived and died and mixed into the mould.

So you will have to use all canniness
To bring this body to its burial
When in your hands I leave what goes in clay;
The wagon that our goods are carried in—
Have it yoked up between the night and day,
And when the breath is from my body gone,
Bear body out, the wagon lay it on;

And cover it with gear that's taken hence—
"The goods of Brendan is what's here," you'll say
To those who'll halt you; they will pass you then:
Tinkers and tailors, soldiers, farmers, smiths,
You'll leave beside their doors—all those thwart men
For whom my virtue was a legacy
That they would profit in, each a degree—

As though it were indeed some chalice, staff,
Crozier, or casket, that they might come to,
And show to those who chanced upon the way,
And have, not knowing how the work was done
In scrolls and figures and in bright inlay:
Whence came the gold and silver that they prize,
The blue enamels and the turquoises!

I, Brendan, had a name came from the sea—
I was the first who sailed the outer main,
And past all forelands and all fastnesses!
I passed the voiceless anchorites, their isles,
Saw the ice-palaces upon the seas,
Mentioned Christ's name to men cut off from men,
Heard the whales snort, and saw the Kraken!

And on a wide-branched, green, and glistening tree
Beheld the birds that had been angels erst:
Between the earth and heaven 'twas theirs to wing:
Fallen from High they were, but they had still
Music of Heaven's Court: I heard them sing:
Even now that island of the unbeached coast
I see, and hear the white, resplendent host!

For this they'd have my burial in this place,
Their hillside, and my resurrection be
Out of the mould that they with me would share.
But I have chosen Cluan for my ground—
A happy place! Some grace came to me there:
And you, as you go towards it, to men say,
Should any ask you on that long highway:

"Brendan is here, who had great saints for friends:
Ita, who reared him on a mother's knee,

Enda, who from his fastness blessed his sail:
Then Brighid, she who had the flaming heart,
And Colum-cille, prime of all the Gael;
Gildas of Britain, wisest child of light."
And saying this, drive through the falling night.

The Ballad of Downal Baun

The moon-cradle's rocking and rocking,
Where a cloud and a cloud goes by:
Silently rocking and rocking,
The moon-cradle out in the sky.

The hound's in his loop by the fire,
The bond-woman spins at the door;
One rides on a horse through the court-yard:
The sword-sheath drops on the floor.

I

My grandfather, Downal Baun,
Had the dream that comes three times:
He dreamt it first when, a servant-boy,
He lay by the nets and the lines,

In the house of Fargal More,
And by Fargal's ash-strewn fire,
When Downal had herded the kine in the waste,
And had foddered them all in the byre;

And he dreamt the dream when he lay
Under sails that were spread to the main,
When he took his rest amid dusky seas,
On the deck of a ship of Spain;

And the dream came to him beneath
The roof he had raised in his pride,
When beside him there lay and dreamt of her kin,
His strange and far-brought bride.

He had dreamt three times of the treasure
That fills a broken tale—
The hoard of the folk who had raised the mounds,
Who had brewed the Heather Ale;

And he knew by the thrice-come dream
He could win that hoard by right,
If he drew it out of the lake by a rush
Upon Saint Brighid's Night,
By rushes strung to the yoke of an ox
That had never a hair of white!

II

So Downal, the silent man,
Went to many a far-off fair,
And he bought him an ox no man could say
Was white by a single hair;

And he came to the edge of the lake
Where no curlew cried overhead:
Silent and bare from the shaking reeds
The lake-waters spread;

And he found it afloat on the current,
The yoke that was hard for the brunt;
And he took the yoke and he bound it,
Upon the ox its front;

It was strung with a tie of rushes:
He saw the burthened net:
By the push of the ox, by the pull on the rush
Towards the shore the hoard was set!

Gold cups for Downal Baun,
Sword hilts that Kings' hands wore!
O the rush-string drew the treasure
Till the ripples touched the shore!

Red rings for Downal's bride,
With silver for her rein!
But weight was laid on each mesh of the net,
And the lake held its own again!

"I will break their strength," he cried,
"Though they put forth all of their might,
For to me was given the yoke and the dream,
And the ox with no hair of white."

He whispered, "Labour, O Creature."
The wide-horned head was set;
The runnels came from eyes, nose and mouth;
The thick hide was all sweat.

"Forgive me the goad, O Creature!"
It hunched from foreleg to flank,
Heaved; then the yoke on its forehead
Split, and the treasure sank,
And Downal was left with the broken yoke,
And the silent ox on the bank.

He turned the ox to the sedges;
He took it and held the yoke up,
Then he flung it far back in the waters
Of the dark mountain-cup;

And he shouted, "Doomsters, I know
Till five score years from this night,

The treasure is lost, and I trow
My ox has the hair of white."

He stood by the ox its front,
And brute and man were still,
Till Downal saw lights burn on the lake,
And fires within the hill.

III

He turned: a horse was beside him;
It was white as his ox was black;
Who rode it was a woman:
She paced with him down the track;

And along a road not straitened
By ridge or tower or wood,
And past where the Stones of Morna
Like headless giants stood;

And then on the Night of Saint Brighid,
The prayer of her vigil he said,
When he looked on the white-horsed woman,
And saw the sign on her head.

"The silks that I wear to my elbows,
The golden clasps at my side,
The silver upon my girdle—
I will give them for your bride."

"Such gear, O Horned Woman,
Makes due a pledge, I deem."
"Nay. I will gift you freely,
And you shall tell your dream."

"They say that whoever tells not
His dream till he hears the birds—
That man will know the prophecies
In long-remembered words."

"Nay. Tell your dream. Then this hazel
Distaff your wife will gain."
"The thing that comes in silence," he said,
"In silence must remain."

"O dream-taught man," said the woman—
She stood where the willows grew,
A woman from the country
Where the cocks never crew!

"O dream-taught man," said the woman—
She stayed by a running stream—
"As wise, as wise as the man," she said,
"Who never told his dream."

Then, swift as the flight of the sea-pie,
White woman, white horse, went away,
And Downal passed his haggard,
And faced the spear of the day;

And brought his ox to the byre,
And gave it a measure of straw—
"A white hair you have," said Downal,
"But my plough you are fit to draw,

"And for no dream you'll be burthened,
And for none you will bear the yoke."
Then he lifted the latch of his house-door,

And his bride at his coming awoke,
And he drank the milk that she gave him,
And the bread she made he broke.

The ox was his help thereafter
When he ploughed the upland and lea,
And the growth on the Ridge of the Black Ox
Had a place in men's memory.

And my grandfather, Downal Baun,
Henceforth grew in gains where he stood—
Strong salmon of Lough Oughter,
Grey hawk of the shady wood!

The moon-cradle's rocking and rocking,
Where a cloud and a cloud goes by:
Silently rocking and rocking,
The moon-cradle out in the sky.

To morrow we'll gather the rushes,
And plait them beside our fire,
And make Saint Brighid's crosses
To hang in the room and the byre.

Polonius and the Ballad Singers

A GAUNT-BUILT woman and her son-in-law,
A broad-faced fellow, with such flesh as shows
Nothing but easy nature, and his wife,
The woman's daughter, who spills all her talk
Out of a wide mouth, but who has eyes as grey
As Connemara, where the mountain-ash
Shows berries red indeed—They enter now,
Our country-singers!

Sing, my good woman, sing us some romance
That has been round our chimney-nooks so long
'Tis nearly native—something blown here
And since made racy—like yon tree, I might say—
Native by influence if not by species—
Shaped by our winds—you understand, I think?

—I'll sing the song, sir—

To-night you see my face—
Maybe never more you'll gaze
On the one that for you left his friends and kin;
For by the hard commands
Of the lord that rules these lands
On a ship I'll be borne from Cruckmaelinn!

Oh, you know your beauty bright
Has made him think delight
More than from any fair one he will gain;
Oh, you know that all his will
Strains and strives around you till
As the hawk upon his hand you are as tame!

56

Then she to him replied:
"I'll no longer you deny,
And I'll let you have the pleasure of my charms,
  For to-night I'll be your bride,
  And whatever may betide
It's we will lie in one another's arms!"

                              You should not sing
With body doubled up and face aside—
There is a climax here—"It's we will lie—"
Hem—passionate!—And what does your daughter sing?

—A song I like when I do climb bare hills—
'Tis all about a hawk—

  No bird that sits on rock or bough
  Has such a front as thine;
  No King that has made war his trade
  Such conquest in his eyne!
  I know thee rock-like on the rock
  Where none can mark a shape;
  I climb, but thou dost climb with wings,
  And like a wish escape,
    She said,
  And like a wish escape!

  No maid that kissed his bonny mouth
  Of another mouth was glad;
  Such pride was in our Chieftain's eyes,
  Such countenance he had!
  But since they made him fly our rocks,
  Thou, Creature, art my quest—
  Then lift me with thy steady eyes,

If then to tear my breast,
  She said,
If then to tear my breast!

                              The songs they have
Are the last relics of the feudal world!
Women will keep them—byzants, doubloons,
When men will take up songs that are as new
As dollar-bills. What song have you, young man?

—A song my father had, sir. It was sent him
From across the sea, and there was letter with it,
Asking my father to put it to a tune
And sing it all roads. He did that, in troth,
And five pounds of tobacco were sent with the song
To fore-reward him. I'll sing it for you now—
"The Baltimore Exile."

  The house I was bred in—ah, does it remain?
  Low walls and loose thatch standing lone in the rain,
  With the clay of the walls coming through in its stain,
  Like the blackbird's left nest in the briar!

  Does a child there give heed to the song of the lark,
  As it lifts and it drops till the fall of the dark,
  When the heavy-foot kine trudge home from the
        paurk,
  Or do none but the red-shank now listen?

  The sloe-bush, I know, grows close to the well,
  And its blossoms long-lasting are there, I can tell,
  When the kid that was yeaned when the first ones befell
  Can jump to the ditch that they grow on!

But there's silence on all. Then do none ever pass
On the way to the fair, or the pattern, or mass?
Do the grey-coated lads drive the ball through the grass
And speed to the sweep of the hurl?

O youths of my land! Then will no Bolivar
Ever muster your ranks for delivering war?
Will your hopes become fixed and beam like a star?
Will they pass like the mist from your fields?

The swan and the swallow, the cuckoo and crake
May visit my land and find hillside and lake,
And I send my song—I'll not see her awake—
I'm a bird too old to uncage now!

A little silver in a little purse!
Take it and spend it on your journey, Friends.

We will. And may we meet your Honor's like
Every day's end!

A song is more lasting than the voice of the birds!

A word is more lasting than the riches of the world!

Old Men Complaining

FIRST OLD MAN

(HE threw his crutched stick down; there came
Into his face the anger flame,
And he spoke viciously of one
Who thwarted him—his son's son.
He turned his head away.) "I hate
Absurdity of language, prate
From growing fellows. We'd not stay
About the house the whole of a day
When we were young,
Keeping no job and giving tongue!

"Not us, in troth! We would no come
For a bit or sup, but stay from home
If we gave answers, or we'd creep
Back to the house, and in we'd peep
Just like a corncrake.

"My grandson and his comrades take
A piece of coal from you, from me
A log, or sod of turf, maybe,
And in some empty place they'll light
A fire, and stay there all night,
A wisp of lads! Now understand
The blades of grass under my hand
Would be destroyed by company!
There's no good company! We go
With what is lowest to the low!
He stays up late, and how can he
Rise early? So he lags in bed
And she is worn to a thread

With calling him—his grandmother—
She's an old woman, and she must make
Stir when the birds are half awake
In dread he'd lose this job like the other!"

SECOND OLD MAN
"They brought yon fellow over here
And set him up for overseer:
Though men from work are turned away,
That thick-necked fellow draws full pay,
Three pounds a week. . . . They let burn down
The timber-yard behind the town
Where work was good, though firemen stand
In boots and brasses big and grand
The crow of a cock away from the place;
And with the yard they let burn, too,
The clock in the tower, the clock I knew
As well as I know the look of my face."

THIRD OLD MAN
"The fellow you spoke of has broken his bounds—
He comes to skulk inside of these grounds;
Behind the bushes he lay down
And stretched full hours in the sun.
He rises now, and like a crane
He looks abroad. He's off again.
Three pounds a week, and still he owes
Money in every street he goes,
Hundreds of pounds where we'd not get
The second shilling of a debt." .

FIRST OLD MAN
"Old age has every impediment,

Vexation and discontent;
The rich have more than we: for bit
The cut of bread and over it
The scrape of hog's lard, and for sup
Warm water in a cup.
But different sorts of feeding breaks
The body more than fasting does
With pains and aches!

"I'm not too badly off, for I
Have pipe and tobacco, a place to lie,
A nook to myself; but from my hand
Is taken the strength to back command,
I'm broken, and there's gone from me
The privilege of authority."

(I heard them speak—
The old men heavy on the sod,
Letting their angers come
Between them and the thought of God!)

Girls Spinning

FIRST GIRL

Mallo lero iss im bo nero!
Go where they're threshing and find me my lover,
Mallo lero iss im bo baun!

SECOND GIRL

Mallo lero iss im bo nero!
Who shall I bring you? Rody the Rover?
Mallo lero iss im bo baun!

FIRST GIRL

Mallo lero iss im bo nero!
Listen and hear what he's singing over.
Mallo lero iss im bo baun!

(*A man's voice sings:*)
I went out in the evening, my sweetheart for to find;
I stood by her cottage window, as well I do mind;
I stood by her cottage window, and I thought I would
    get in,
But instead of pleasures for me my sorrows did begin!

Fine colour had my darling though it wasn't me was
    there:
I did not sit beside her, but inside there was a pair!
I stood outside the window like a poor neglected soul,
And I waited till my own name was brought across the
    coal!

Here's a health unto the blackbird that sings upon the
    tree,

And here's to the willy-wagtail that goes the road with
    me!
Here's a health unto my darling and to them she makes
    her own:
She's deserving of good company; for me, I go my lone.

My love she is courteous and handsome and tall;
For wit and for behaviour she's foremost of them all!
She says she is in no way bound, that with me she'll go
    free,
But my love has too many lovers to have any love for me!

FIRST GIRL
Mallo lero iss im bo nero!
Who weds him might cry with the wandering plover!
Mallo lero iss im bo baun!

Mallo lero iss im bo nero!
Where they're breaking the horses, go find me my lover!
Mallo lero iss im bo baun!

SECOND GIRL
Mallo lero iss im bo nero!
Him with the strong hand I will bring from the clover.
Mallo lero iss im bo baun!

FIRST GIRL
Mallo lero iss im bo nero!
I wait till I hear what he's singing over.
Mallo lero iss im bo baun!

(*Another man's voice:*)
Are they not the good men of Eirinn,
Who give not their thought nor their voice

To fortune, but take without dowry
The maids of their choice?

For the trout has sport in the river
Whether prices be up or low-down,
And the salmon, he slips through the water
Not heeding the town!

Then if she, the love of my bosom
Did laugh as she stood by my door,
O I'd rise then and draw her in to me,
With kisses *go leor!*

It's not likely the wind in the tree-tops
Would trouble our love nor our rest,
Nor the hurrying footsteps would draw her,
My love from my breast!

FIRST GIRL

Mallo lero iss im bo nero!
He sings to the *girsha* in the hazel-wood cover.
Mallo lero iss im bo baun!

Mallo lero iss im bo nero!
Go where they're shearing and find me my lover.
Mallo lero iss im bo baun!

SECOND GIRL

Mallo lero iss im bo nero!
The newly-come youth is looking straight over!
Mallo lero iss im bo baun!

FIRST GIRL

Mallo lero iss im bo nero!

If you mind what he sings you'll have silver trover.
Mallo lero iss im bo baun!

(*A young man's voice sings:*)
Once I went over the ocean,
On a ship that was bound for proud Spain:
Some people were singing and dancing,
But I had a heart full of pain.

I'll put now a sail on the lake
That's between my treasure and me,
And I'll sail over the lake
Till I come to the Joyce country.

She'll hear my boat on the shingles,
And she'll hear my step on the land,
And the corncrake deep in the meadow
Will tell her that I'm at hand!

The summer comes to Glen Nefin
With heavy dew on the leas,
With the gathering of wild honey
To the tops of all the trees;

In honey and dew the summer
Upon the ground is shed,
And the cuckoo cries until dark
Where my *storeen* has her bed!

And if O'Hanlon's daughter
Will give me a welcome kind,
O never will my sail be turned
To a harsh and a heavy wind!

FIRST GIRL

Mallo lero iss im bo nero!
Welcome I'll give him over and over.
Mallo lero iss im bo baun!

Blades

SOJOURNER, set down
Your skimming wheel;
Nothing is sharp
That we have of steel:
Nothing has edge:—
Oh, whirl around
Your wheel of stone
Till our blades be ground!

Harshly, quickly, under blades
Hafted with horn and wood and bone
Went the wheel:
Narrow long knives that should be one edge,
House-knives that sliced the loaf to the heel,
And scraped scales off mackerel,
And weighty knives that were shaped like a wedge—
Stone wakened keenness in their steel:
Knives with which besom-makers pare
Their heather-stalks, and hawkers' blades
Used by men of a dozen trades;
Broad-bladed knives that cut bacon-sides,
And stumpy knives for cobblers' hides,
With hunters' knives that were thinned with wear:—
All were brought to,
All were laid on,
All were ground by
The Sojourner's wheel.

And those who filled the market-square
Saw hand and eye upon their ware
That were well schooled and scrupulous

To spend upon that task their use.
But sparks came from the eyes and met
The sparks that were from the edges whet
As eagerly and wittingly
The dullness of each blade scoured he,
And the brow he bent was like a stone.

Over the grinding-stone he sang,
"The dalesman's sword shall make you fear,
And the dirk in the grasp of the mountaineer,
And likewise the pirate's blue cutlass
Who have left your blades long edgeless!"
But the men were thinking of games of cards,
And the looks of the boys were turned towards
The corner where they played pitch and toss,
And the women thought of the herring across
The tongs to roast where pot-hooks hang.
"Unready and unforward men
Who have no right to any lien
On the gifts of Tubal Cain,
The gifts of our father, Tubal Cain!"

But no one drew meaning from the song
As he made an equal edge along
One side of the blade and the other one,
And polished the surface till it shone.

"Now leave a blessing on what you have done."

"For what I have done I take my fee,
But no blessing I leave on it," said he,
"Everybody knows,
Everybody knows

That the knife-grinder
No blessing bestows."

Then the market-place, with wheel a-pack,
He left, and the men to their cards went back
And talked of a bird in the cocker's loft;
And of liming linnets beside the croft
The boys told between pitch and toss;
And the women laid the herring across
The tongs to roast for a sloven's meal.

And he went out beside the Peel
Tower, and through Saint Selskar's Gate,
Heading at a hearty rate
Towards the hilltops and the shades.

And three who brought back sharpened blades
To their fathers' stalls by the Tan-yard Side,
And then stayed while a blackbird cried
Quietly by their groundsills—
The butcher's daughter,
The cobbler's daughter,
The hawker's daughter,
Were lost on the hills!

Scanderbeg

SHE sat on the wall and dangled her silk-stockinged legs,
Saying, "I'll not have them stung for any old man who is
    dead,"
So I went where nettles were rank and came on a stone
    that read,
"Matthew de Rienzi,
Knight, born in Germany,
Descended from George Castriot, alias Scanderbeg,
Who fifty-two battles waged with conquest against the
    Great Turk."
More: the Knight de Rienzi,
Learned in Irish, composed for it a Dictionary,
Corresponded with men of state upon affairs,
And died here; fifty-seven his years—
Peace be with Matthew!
Then I looked where she sat on the wall dangling her
    silk-stockinged legs,
Which she would not have stung for any old man who
    was dead,
As she said—
Not even, I supposed, for a descendant of Scanderbeg!
But I heard a curlew
Over the river beside me, the Shannon it was,
And saw from that to the Danube, and it was crossed
By turbaned men under whose stallions' hooves the grass
Never grew again;
And that battlefield, the Plain of the Blackbirds, Kossovo,
And the Sultan Murad slain,
And the breach in Constantinople's wall, and Belgrade,
Buda and Vienna under great cannonade,

And the sweep of the Pashas onward till Hungary, Poland,
　　the Germanies were all dismayed,
And that historyless man, George Castriot, holding at bay
Byzantium's conquerors in the mountains of Albania;
Then battles along the Rhine,
And Dutchmen and English, Frenchmen and Irish, forc-
　　ing or holding this line,
And the Shannon crossed and Aughrim lost to our own
　　overthrow!
Two hundred years' battling in Europe at the name of
　　Scanderbeg
Spun through my mind as a curlew cried overhead!

Minoan

O WHAT a hound he has! A hound so high
Might follow Talos, him, the Bronzen Man,
And fill the Labyrinth with just a cry!
As bronze-topped spear his height, and there, besides,
A horse that bends a neck that's like a bride's!

The slim horse stands behind: the horse's mane
Is dizened into little candle flames,
And you can tell the hound's not yet a-strain—
He dreams of chasing eagles in the wind;
But thin-flanked bulls are on his master's mind!

The sun is up; the grasses trampled o'er
Still keep the freshness of the creature gone;
He holds the leash; clear spaces are before!
Oh, Youth will be away with all he sees
From Knossos and the Daedal Palaces!

Indian

Where has she come from, that fawn? The hermit with
    hair and with beard
Earthy, like roots of the trees, looks at her from under his
    brows.

The bride of the hero is there; her hands are filled with
    the blooms
Of the mango and champak trees: her long eyes look on
    the fawn.

She sees through the ages gone, and side by side with that
    fawn
Herself, and they move through the glades where the
    mango and champak bloom.

But a bow stands out from the trees:
The hero, hardly beheld, has his hands on the shaft and
    the bow.

Where has she come from, that fawn? As though on lotos
    she'd lain
Her skin is patterned o'er; like a moonray she moves
    through the glade.

The fawn shows her moonray grace; she moves with her
    head upraised.
The cord is strained in his grasp. To meet that shaft she
    has come.

Hawaiian

SANDALWOOD, you say, and in your thoughts it chimes
With Tyre and Solomon; to me it rhymes
With places bare upon Pacific mountains,
With spaces empty in the minds of men.

Sandalwood!
The Kings of Hawaii call out their men,
The men go up the mountains in files;
Hands that knew only the stone axe now wield the iron
    axe:
The sandalwood trees go down.

More sandalwood is called for:
The men who hunt the whale will buy sandalwood;
The Kings would change canoes for ships.
Men come down from the mountains carrying sandal-
    wood on their backs;
More and more men are levied;
They go up the mountains in files; they leave their taro-
    patches so that famine comes down on the land.

But this sandalwood grows upon other trees, a parasite;
It needs a growing thing to grow upon;
Its seed and its soil are not enough for it!

Too greedy are the Kings;
Too eager are the men who hunt the whale to sail to
    Canton with fragrant wood to make shrines for the
    Buddhas;
Too sharp is the iron axe!

Nothing will ever bring together again
The spores and the alien sap that nourished them,
The trees and the trees they would plant themselves
    upon:
Like the myths of peoples,
Like the faiths of peoples,
Like the speech of peoples,
Like the ancient creation chants,
The sandalwood is gone!

A fragrance in shrines—
But the trees will never live again!

WILD EARTH

TO

A. E.

WHO FOSTERED ME

The Plougher

Sunset and silence! A man; around him earth savage,
    earth broken;
Beside him two horses, a plough!

Earth savage, earth broken, the brutes, the dawn-man
    there in the sunset,
And the plough that is twin to the sword, that is founder
    of cities!

"Brute-tamer, plough-maker, earth-breaker! Canst hear?
    There are ages between us—
Is it praying you are as you stand there alone in the
    sunset?

Surely our sky-born gods can be nought to you, earth
    child and earth-master—
Surely your thoughts are of Pan, or of Wotan, or Dana?

Yet why give thought to the gods? Has Pan led your
    brutes where they stumble?
Has Dana numbed pain of the child-bed, or Wotan put
    hands to your plough?

What matter your foolish reply! O man standing lone
    and bowed earthward,
Your task is a day near its close. Give thanks to the night-
    giving god."

Slowly the darkness falls, the broken lands blend with the
    savage;
The brute-tamer stands by the brutes, a head's breadth
    only above them.

A head's breadth? Aye, but therein is hell's depth and the
    height up to heaven,
And the thrones of the gods and their halls, their chariots,
    purples, and splendours.

The Furrow and the Hearth

I

STRIDE the hill, Sower,
Up to the sky ridge,
Flinging the seed,
Scattering, exultant!
Mouthing great rhythms
To the long sea-beats
On the wide shore, behind
The ridge of the hillside.

Below in the darkness—
The slumber of mothers,
The cradles at rest,
The fire-seed sleeping
Deep in white ashes!

Give to darkness and sleep,
O Sower, O Seer!
Give me to the earth—
With the seed I would enter!
Oh, the growth through the silence
From strength to new strength;
Then the strong bursting forth
Against primal forces,
To laugh in the sunshine,
To gladden the world!

II

Who will bring the red fire
Unto a new hearth?

Who will lay the wide stone
On the waste of the earth?

Who is fain to begin
To build day by day—
To raise up his house
Of the moist yellow clay?

There's clay for the making
Moist in the pit,
There are horses to trample
The rushes through it.

Above where the wild duck
Arise up and fly,
There one can build
To the wind and the sky.

There are boughs in the forest
To pluck young and green,
O'er them thatch of the crop
Shall be heavy and clean.

I speak unto him
Who in dead of the night
Sees the red streaks
In the ash deep and white;

While around him he hears
Men stir in their rest,
And the stir of the babe
That is close to the breast!

He shall arise,
He shall go forth alone,
Lay stone on the earth,
And bring fire to stone.

A Drover

To Meath of the pastures,
From wet hills by the sea,
Through Leitrim and Longford,
Go my cattle and me.

I hear in the darkness
Their slipping and breathing—
I name them the by-ways
They're to pass without heeding;

Then the wet, winding roads,
Brown bogs with black water,
And my thoughts on white ships
And the King o' Spain's daughter.

O farmer, strong farmer!
You can spend at the fair,
But your face you must turn
To your crops and your care;

And soldiers, red soldiers!
You've seen many lands,
But you walk two by two,
And by captain's commands!

O the smell of the beasts,
The wet wind in the morn,
And the proud and hard earth
Never broken for corn!

And the crowds at the fair,
The herds loosened and blind,

Loud words and dark faces,
And the wild blood behind!

(O strong men with your best
I would strive breast to breast,
I could quiet your herds
With my words, with my words!)

I will bring you, my kine,
Where there's grass to the knee,
But you'll think of scant croppings
Harsh with salt of the sea.

A Connachtman

It's my fear that my wake won't be quiet,
Nor my wake house a silent place:
For who would keep back the hundreds
Who would touch my breast and my face?

For the good men were always my friends,
From Galway back into Clare;
In strength, in sport, and in spending,
I was foremost at the fair;

In music, in song, and in friendship,
In contests by night and by day,
By all who knew it was given to me
That I bore the branch away.

Now let Manus Joyce, my friend
(If he be at all in the place),
Make smooth the boards of the coffin
They will put above my face.

The old men will have their stories
Of all the deeds in my days,
And the young men will stand by the coffin,
And be sure and clear in my praise.

But the girls will stay near the door,
And they'll have but little to say:
They'll bend their heads, the young girls,
And for a while they will pray.

And, going home in the dawning,
They'll be quiet with the boys;

The girls will walk together,
And seldom they'll lift the voice;

And then, between daybreak and dark,
And between the hill and the sea,
Three women, come down from the mountain,
Will raise the keen over me.

But 'tis my grief that I will not hear
When the cuckoo cries in Glenart,
That the wind that lifts when the sails are loosed,
Will never lift my heart.

A Man Bereaved

My wife and my comrade
Will not come at all
Though the pine-tree shall flourish,
The green rush grow tall,
And its cone to the ground
The larch-tree let fall.

She'll not cross my threshold,
Nor with me abide,
Sit down on this doorstep,
Nor lie by my side;
And I'll not hear her sounding
Songs over the din,
Where the people are crowded,
The harvest being in;
Nor see her come lilting
From the field or the fold,
Nor plaiting her long locks
In the young moon nor old.

No more to the hill-tops
Have I heart to go,
Nor to walk through the woods
When the summer sun's low:
Though I weary with delving,
With driving the plough,
I lie on a bed
Sleep has gone from now.

Though goats to their time come
With nobody there;

Though the watched heifer calve
With none to take care,
From the churchyard my woman
Home never will fare.

My house is encumbered,
Unswept my hearth-stone,
The cows low for their milking
In the full height of noon,
No garb is made newly,
No wool is yet spun;
On the floor and untended
Stands the youngling, my son.

On the hills they cry ba-ba,
And bring back their dam;
On the floor and unanswered
Stands the youngling, my lamb,
While I'm saying over
That she'll not come at all
Though the pine-tree shall flourish,
The green rush grow tall,
And its cone to the ground
The larch-tree let fall!

An Old Woman of the Roads

Oh, to have a little house!
To own the hearth and stool and all!
The heaped-up sods upon the fire,
The pile of turf against the wall!

To have a clock with weights and chains
And pendulum swinging up and down,
A dresser filled with shining delph,
Speckled and white and blue and brown!

I could be busy all the day
Clearing and sweeping hearth and floor,
And fixing on their shelf again
My white and blue and speckled store!

I could be quiet there at night
Beside the fire and by myself,
Sure of a bed and loth to leave
The ticking clock and the shining delph!

Och! but I'm weary of mist and dark,
And roads where there's never a house nor bush,
And tired I am of bog and road,
And the crying wind and the lonesome hush!

And I am praying to God on high,
And I am praying him night and day,
For a little house, a house of my own—
Out of the wind's and the rain's way.

Interior

THE little moths are creeping
Across the cottage pane;
On the floor the chickens gather,
And they make talk and complain.

And she sits by the fire
Who has reared so many men;
Her voice is low like the chickens'
With the things she says again:

"The sons that come back do be restless,
They search for the thing to say;
Then they take thought like the swallows,
And the morrow brings them away.

In the old, old days upon Innish,
The fields were lucky and bright,
And if you lay down you'd be covered
By the grass of one soft night.

And doves flew with every burial
That went to Innishore—
Two white doves with the coffened,
But the doves fly no more."

She speaks and the chickens gather,
And they make talk and complain,
While the little moths are creeping
Across the cottage pane.

What the Shuiler Said as She Lay By the Fire in the Farmer's House

I'M glad to lie on a sack of leaves
By a wasted fire and take my ease.
For the wind would strip me bare as a tree—
The wind would blow oul' age upon me,
And I'm dazed with the wind, the rain, and the cold!
If I had only the good red gold
To buy me the comfort of a roof,
And under the thatch the brown of the smoke!
I'd lie up in my painted room
Until my hired girl would come;
And when the sun had warmed my walls
I'd rise up in my silks and shawls,
And break my fast beside the fire.
And I'd watch them that had to sweat
And shiver for shelter and what they ate—
The farmer digging in the fields,
The beggars going from gate to gate,
The horses striving with their loads,
And all the sights upon the roads.

I'd live my lone without clan nor care,
And none around me to crave a share:
The young have mocking, impudent ways,
And I'd never let them a-nigh my place,
And a child has often a pitiful face.
I'd give the rambling fiddler rest,
And for me he would play his best,
And he'd have something to tell of me
From the Moat of Granard down to the sea!
And, though I'd keep distant, I'd let in

Oul' women who would card and spin,
And clash with me, and I'd hear it said,
"Mór, who used to carry her head
As if she was a lady bred,
Has little enough in her house, they say;
And such a one's child I saw on the way
Scaring crows from a crop, and glad to get
In a warmer house, the bit to eat—
Oh, none are safe and none secure,
And it's well for some whose bit is sure!"

I'd never grudge them the weight of their lands
If I had only the good red gold
To huggle between my breast and my hands!

Spinning Songs

(A Young Girl sings it)

THE Lannan Shee
Watched the young man Brian
Cross over the stile towards his father's door,
And she said, "No help,
For now he'll see
His byre, his bawn, and his threshing-floor!
And, oh, the swallows
Forget all wonders
When walls with the nests rise up once more!"
My strand is knit.

"Out of the dream
Of me, into
The round of his labour he will grow;
To spread his fields
In the winds of spring,
And tramp the heavy glebe and sow;
And cut and clamp
And rear the turf
Until the season when they mow."
My wheel runs smooth.

"And while he toils
In field and bog
He will be anxious in his mind
About the thatch
Of barn and rick

94

Against the reiving autumn wind,
And how to make
His gap and gate
Secure against the thieving kind."
  My wool is fine.

"He has gone back;
No more I'll see
Mine image in his deepening eyes;
Then I'll lean above
The Well of the Bride,
And with my beauty, peace will rise!
O autumn star
In a lake well hid,
Fill up my heart and make me wise!"
  My quick brown wheel!

"The women bring
Their pitchers here
At the time when the stir of the house is o'er;
They'll see my face
In the well-water,
And they'll never lift their pitchers more.
For each will say
'How beautiful—
Why should I labour any more!
Indeed I come
Of a race so fine
'Twere waste to labour any more!'"
  My thread is spun.

AN ISLAND SPINNING SONG
(*An Older Girl sings it*)

One came before her and said, beseeching,
"I have fortune and I have lands,
And if you'll share in the goods of my household
All my treasure's at your commands."

But she said to him, "The goods you proffer
Are far from my mind as the silk of the sea!
The arms of him, my young love, round me,
Is all the treasure that's true for me!"

"Proud you are, then, proud of your beauty,
But beauty's a flower will soon decay;
The fairest flowers they bloom in the summer,
They bloom one summer, and they fade away."

"My heart is sad, then, for the little flower
That must so wither where fair it grew—
He who has my heart in keeping,
I would he had my body too."

A MIDLAND SPINNING SONG
(*An Old Woman sings it*)

There was an oul' trooper went riding by
On the road to Carricknabauna,
And sorrow is better to sing than cry
On the way to Carricknabauna!
And as this oul' trooper went riding on
He heard this sung by a crone, a crone
On the road to Carricknabauna!

96

"I'd spread my cloak for you, young lad,
Were it only the breadth of a farthen,
And if your mind was as good as your word,
In troth, it's you I'd rather!
In dread of ere forgetting this,
And before we go any farther,
Hoist me up to the top of the hill,
And show me Carricknabauna!"

"Carricknabauna, Carricknabauna,
Would you show me Carricknabauna?
I lost a horse at Cruckmaelinn,
At the Cross of Bunratty I dropped a limb,
But I left my youth on the crown of the hill
Over by Carricknabauna!"
   Girls, young girls, the rush-light is done.
   What will I do till my thread is spun?

The Knitters

In companies or lone
They bend their heads, their hands
They busy with their gear,
Accomplishing the stitch
That turns the stocking-heel,
Or closes up the toe,
   These knitters at their doors.
Their talk 's of nothing else
But what was told before
Sundown and gone sundown,
While goats bleat from the hill,
And men are tramping home,
   By knitters at their doors.
And we who go this way
A benediction take
From hands that ply this task
For the ten thousandth time—
   Of knitters at their doors.
Since we who deem our days
Most varied, come to own
That all the works we do
Repeat a wonted toil:
May it be done as theirs
Who turn the stocking-heel,
And close the stocking-toe,
With grace and in content,
   These knitters at their doors.

Folding Hour

Now comes the lad with the hazel,
And the folding star 's in the rack;
"Night 's a good herd," to the cattle
He sings, "she brings all things back."

But the bond-woman near to the boorie
Sings with a heart grown wild
How a hundred rivers are flowing
Between herself and her child.

"The geese, even they, trudge homeward
That have their wings and the waste;
Let your thoughts go with night the herder
And be folded for a space."

The Terrible Robber Men

Oh I wish the sun was bright in the sky,
And the fox was back in his den O!
For always I'm hearing the passing by
Of the terrible robber men O!
  Of the terrible robber men.

Oh what does the fox carry over the rye,
When it's bright in the morn again O!
And what is it making the lonesome cry
With the terrible robber men O!
  With the terrible robber men.

Oh I wish the sun was bright in the sky,
And the fox was back in his den O!
For always I'm hearing the passing by
Of the terrible robber men O!
  With the terrible robber men.

Garadh

For the poor body that I own
I could weep many a tear:
The days have stolen flesh and bone,
And left a changling here.

Four feeble bones are left to me,
And the basket of my breast,
And I am mean and ugly now
As the scald flung from the nest.

The briars drag me at the knee,
The brambles go within,
And often do I feel him turn,
The old man in my skin.

The strength is carded from my bones,
The swiftness drained from me,
And all the living thoughts I had
Are like far ships at sea!

The Tin-Whistle Player

'Tis long since, long since, since I heard
A tin-whistle played,
And heard the tunes, the ha'penny tunes
That nobody made!

The tunes that were before Cendfind
And Cir went Ireland's rounds—
That were before the surety
That strings have given sounds!

And now is standing in the mist,
And jigging backward there,
Shrilling with fingers and with breath,
A tin-whistle player!

He has hare's eyes, a long face rimmed
Around with badger-grey;
Aimless, like cries of mountain birds
The tunes he has to play—

The tunes that are for stretches bare,
And men whose lives are lone—
And I had seen that face of his
Sculptured on cross of stone,
That long face, in a place of graves
With nettles overgrown.

A Mountaineer

Ere Beowulf's song
Was heard from the ships,
Ere Roland had set
The horn to his lips:

In Ogham strokes
A name was writ:
That name his name
Lives in yet.

The strokes on the edge
Of the stone might count
The acres he has
On this bare mount;

But he remembers
The pillar-stone,
And knows that he is
Of the seed of Eoin.

AUTUMN

A GOOD stay-at-home season is Autumn: then there's
    work to be joined in by all:
Though the fawns, where the brackens make covert, may
    range away undeterred,
The stags that were lone upon hillocks now give heed to
    the call,
To the bellowing call of the hinds, and they draw back
    to the herd.

A good stay-at-home season is Autumn; the brown world's
    marked into fields;
The corn is up to its growth; the acorns teem in the
    wood;
By the side of the down-fallen fort even the thorn-bush
    yields
A crop, and there by the rath the hazel nuts drop from
    a load.

SPRING

Now, coming on Spring, the days will be growing,
And after Saint Bride's Day my sail I will throw;
Since the thought has come to me I fain would be going,
Till I stand in the middle of the County Mayo!

The first of my days will be spent in Claremorris,
And in Balla, beside it, I'll have drinking and sport,
To Kiltimagh, then, I will go on a visit,
And there, I can tell you, a month will be short.

I solemnly swear that the heart in me rises,
As the wind rises up and the mists break below,

When I think upon Carra, and on Gallen down from it,
The Bush of the Mile, and the Plains of Mayo!

Killeadean's my village, and every good's in it;
The rasp and blackberry to set to one's tooth;
And if Raftery stood in the midst of his people,
Old age would go from him, and he'd step to his youth!

Shall I Go Bound and You Go Free?

SHALL I go bound and you go free,
And love one so removed from me?
Not so; the falcon o'er my brow
Hath better quest, I dare avow!

And must I run where you will ride,
And must I stay where you abide?
Not so; the feather that I wear
Is from an eyrie in the air!

And must I climb a broken stair,
And must I pace a chamber bare?
Not so; the Brenny plains are wide
And there are banners where I ride!

She Moved Through the Fair

My young love said to me, "My brothers won't mind,
And my parents won't slight you for your lack of kind."
Then she stepped away from me, and this she did say
"It will not be long, love, till our wedding day."

She stepped away from me and she moved through the
    fair,
And fondly I watched her go here and go there,
Then she went her way homeward with one star awake,
As the swan in the evening moves over the lake.

The people were saying no two were ere wed
But one had a sorrow that never was said,
And I smiled as she passed with her goods and her gear,
And that was the last that I saw of my dear.

I dreamt it last night that my young love came in,
So softly she entered, her feet made no din;
She came close beside me, and this she did say
"It will not be long, love, till our wedding day."

Across the Door

THE fiddles were playing and playing,
The couples were out on the floor;
From converse and dancing he drew me,
And across the door.

Ah! strange were the dim, wide meadows,
And strange was the cloud-strewn sky,
And strange in the meadows the corncrakes,
And they making cry!

The hawthorn bloom was by us,
Around us the breath of the south—
White hawthorn, strange in the night-time—
His kiss on my mouth!

A Cradle Song

O, MEN from the fields!
Come gently within.
Tread softly, softly,
O! men coming in.

Mavourneen is going
From me and from you,
Where Mary will fold him
With mantle of blue!

From reek of the smoke
And cold of the floor,
And the peering of things
Across the half-door.

O, men from the fields!
Soft, softly come through—
Mary puts round him
Her mantle of blue.

The Sister's Lullaby

You would not slumber
If laid at my breast:
   You would not slumber.

The river-flood beats
The swan from her nest:
   You would not slumber.

And like that quick flood
My blood goes unguessed:
   You would not slumber.

Times without number
Has called the wood quest:
   Times without number.

As oft as she called
To me you were pressed:
   Times without number.

Now you'd not slumber
If laid at my breast
   Times without number.

O starling reed-resting,
I'll rock you to rest:
   So you will slumber.

The Beggar's Child

Mavourneen, we'll go far away
From the net of the crooked town
Where they grudge us the light of the day.

Around my neck you will lay
Two tight little arms of brown.
Mavourneen, we'll go far away
From the net of the crooked town.

And what will we hear on the way?
The stir of wings up and down
In nests where the little birds stay!
Mavourneen, we'll go far away
From the net of the crooked town
Where they grudge us the light of the day.

No Child

I HEARD in the night the pigeons
Stirring within their nest:
The wild pigeons' stir was tender,
Like a child's hand at the breast.

I cried "O stir no more!
(My breast was touched with tears).
O pigeons, make no stir—
A childless woman hears."

An Drinaun Donn

A HUNDRED men think I am theirs when with them I
   drink ale,
But their presence fades away from me and their high
   spirits fail
When I think upon your converse kind by the meadow
   and the linn,
And your form smoother than the silk on the Mountain
   of O'Flynn.

Oh, Paddy, is it pain to you that I'm wasting night and
   day,
And, Paddy, is it grief to you that I'll soon be in the
   clay?
My first love with the winning mouth, my treasure you'll
   abide,
Till the narrow coffin closes me and the grass grows
   through my side.

The man who strains to leap the wall, we think him
   foolish still,
When to his hand is the easy ditch to vault across at
   will;
The rowan tree is fine and high, but bitter its berries
   grow,
While blackberries and raspberries are on shrubs that
   blossom low.

Farewell, farewell, forever, to yon town amongst the
   trees;
Farewell, the town that draws me on mornings and on
   eves.

Oh, many's the ugly morass now, and many's the crooked
    road,
That lie henceforth between me and where my heart's
    bestowed.

And Mary, Ever Virgin, where will I turn my head!
I know not where his house is built, nor where his fields
    are spread.
Ah, kindly was the counsel that my kinsfolk gave to me,
"The hundred twists are in his heart, and the thousand
    tricks has he."

The Poor Girl's Meditation

I AM sitting here
Since the moon rose in the night,
Kindling a fire,
And striving to keep it alight;
The folk of the house are lying
In slumber deep;
The geese will be gabbling soon:
The whole of the land is asleep.

May I never leave this world
Until my ill-luck is gone;
Till I have cows and sheep,
And the lad that I love for my own;
I would not think it long,
The night I would lie at his breast,
And the daughters of spite, after that,
Might say the thing they liked best.

Love takes the place of hate,
If a girl have beauty at all:
On a bed that was narrow and high,
A three-month I lay by the wall:
When I bethought on the lad
That I left on the brow of the hill,
I wept from dark until dark,
And my cheeks have the tear-tracks still.

And, O young lad that I love,
I am no mark for your scorn;
All you can say of me is
Undowered I was born:

And if I've no fortune in hand,
Nor cattle and sheep of my own,
This I can say, O lad,
I am fitted to lie my lone!

Dermott Donn MacMorna

ONE day you'll come to my husband's door,
  Dermott Donn MacMorna,
One day you'll come to Hugh's dark door,
And the pain at my heart will be no more,
  Dermott Donn MacMorna!

From his bed, from his fire I'll rise,
  Dermott Donn MacMorna,
From the bed of Hugh, from his fire I'll rise,
With my laugh for the pious, the quiet, the wise,
  Dermott Donn MacMorna!

Lonesome, lonesome, the house of Hugh,
  Dermott Donn MacMorna,
No cradle rocks in the house of Hugh;
The list'ning fire has thought of you,
  Dermott Donn MacMorna!

Out of this loneliness we'll go,
  Dermott Donn MacMorna,
Together at last we two will go
Down a darkening road with a gleam below,
Ah, but the winds do bitter blow,
  Dermott Donn MacMorna!

A Poor Scholar of the 'Forties

My eyelids red and heavy are
With bending o'er the smold'ring peat.
I know the Æneid now by heart,
My Virgil read in cold and heat,
In loneliness and hunger smart.
    And I know Homer, too, I ween,
    As Munster poets know Ossian.

And I must walk this road that winds
'Twixt bog and bog, while east there lies
A city with its men and books;
With treasures open to the wise,
Heart-words from equals, comrade-looks;
    Down here they have but tale and song,
    They talk Repeal the whole night long.

"You teach Greek verbs and Latin nouns,"
The dreamer of Young Ireland said,
"You do not hear the muffled call,
The sword being forged, the far-off tread
Of hosts to meet as Gael and Gall—
    What good to us your wisdom-store,
    Your Latin verse, your Grecian lore?"

And what to me is Gael or Gall?
Less than the Latin or the Greek—
I teach these by the dim rush-light
In smoky cabins night and week.
But what avail my teaching slight?
    Years hence, in rustic speech, a phrase,
    As in wild earth a Grecian vase!

A Saint

THE stir of children with fresh dresses on,
And men who meet and say unguarded words,
And women from the coops
Of drudgeries released;

And standing at their doors to watch go by
Small pomps with pennons and with first spring-flowers,
And, lifted over them,
Your name that sanctifies.

But you, when you came here, it was to front
Hard-handed men, and trouble them for dues
To stay the fatherless—
Portion of what they ploughed.

To claim resource from them whose own resource
Was pittance—this you came here to do,
And give for what you gained
Your season of bright youth:

The hunt upon the mountain-side, the dance
Down in the vale; the whisper at the door;
Kiss on unstaying lips
That afterwards would stay;

Music you could have made would make our land
Of noble note and join our different breeds,
And make your name endeared
On roadside and in hall.

All this was changed, as when the warm stream
Setting through ocean toward vine-bearing isles,

Turns its flow toward capes
Where heather only thrives.

That day that was of battles and hard pledges
Has all been changed into this whitened morn—
Music and holiday,
And benediction bells.

The Toy-Maker

I AM the Toy-maker; I have brought from the town
As much in my plack as should fetch a whole crown,
I'll array for you now my stock of renown
And man's the raree will show you.

Here's a horse that is rearing to bound through the smoke
Of cannon and musket, and, face to that ruck,
The horseman with sword ready-held for the stroke,
Lord Lucan, maybe, or Prince Charlie.

An old woman sitting and waiting for call,
With her baskets of cockles and apples and all;
A one-legged sailor attending a ball,
And a tailor and nailer busy.

Or would you have these? A goose ganging by,
With head up in challenge to all who come nigh;
A cock with a comb dangling over his eye,
And a hen on a clutch nicely sitting;

Or a duck that is chasing a quick thing around,
Or a crow that is taking three hops on the ground,
Or an ass with head down (he is held in a pound);
Or a fox with his tail curled around him?

A ship made of shells that have sheen of the sea,
All ready to sail for black Barbarie,
The Lowlands of Holland, or High Germanie—
And who'll be the one that will steer her?

I'll speak of my trade: there's a day beyond day
When the hound needn't hunt and the priest needn't pray,

And the clerk needn't write, and the hen needn't lay,
Whence come all the things that I show you.

I am the Toy-maker; upon the town wall
My crib is high up; I have down-look on all,
And coach and wheelbarrow I carve in my stall,
Making things with no troubles in them.

A Ballad Maker

ONCE I loved a maiden fair,
Over the hills and far away,
Lands she had and lovers to spare,
Over the hills and far away.
And I was stooped and troubled sore,
And my face was pale, and the coat I wore
Was thin as my supper the night before
Over the hills and far away.

Once I passed in the Autumn late,
Over the hills and far away,
Her bawn and barn and painted gate,
Over the hills and far away.
She was leaning there in the twilight space,
Sweet sorrow was on her fair young face,
And her wistful eyes were away from the place,
Over the hills and far away.

Maybe she thought as she watched me come,
Over the hills and far away,
With my awkward stride and my face so glum,
Over the hills and far away.
Spite of his stoop, he still is young,
They say he goes the Shee among,
Ballads he makes; I've heard them sung
Over the hills and far away.

She gave me good-night in gentle wise,
Over the hills and far away,
Shyly lifting to mine, dark eyes,
Over the hills and far away.

What could I do but stop and speak,
And she no longer proud, but meek?
She plucked me a rose like her wild-rose cheek—
Over the hills and far away.

To-morrow Mavourneen a sleeveen weds,
Over the hills and far away,
With corn in haggard and cattle in sheds,
Over the hills and far away.
And I who have lost her, the dear, the rare—
Well, I got me this ballad to sing at the fair,
'Twill bring enough money to drown my care,
Over the hills and far away.

The Poet

"The blackbird's in the briar,
The seagull's on the ground—
They are nests, and they're more than nests," he said,
"They are tokens I have found.

There, where the rain-dashed briar
Marks an empty glade,
The blackbird's nest is seen," he said,
"Clay-rimmed, uncunningly made.

By shore of the inland lake,
Where surgeless water shoves,
The seagulls have their nests," he said,
"As low as cattles' hooves."

I heard a poet say it,
The sojourner of a night;
His head was up to the rafter,
Where he stood in candles' light.

"Your houses are like the seagulls'
Nests—they are scattered and low;
Like the blackbirds' nests in briars," he said,
"Uncunningly made—even so.

But close to the ground are reared
The wings that have widest sway,
And the birds that sing best in the wood," he said,
"Were reared with breasts to the clay.

You've wildness—I've turned it to song;
You've strength—I've turned it to wings;

The welkin's for your conquest then,
The wood to your music rings."

I heard a poet say it,
The sojourner of a night;
His head was up to the rafter,
Where he stood in candles' light.

OTHER LANDS AND SEAS

TO

SARAH PURSER

Arab Songs

I. THE PARROT AND THE FALCON

My Afghan poet-friend
  With this made his message end,
"The scroll around my wall shows two the poets have known—
  The parrot and falcon they—
  The parrot hangs on his spray,
And silent the falcon sits with brooding and baleful eyes.

Men come to me: one says
  'We have given your verses praise,
And we will keep your name abreast of the newer names;
  But you must make what accords
  With poems that are household words—
Your own: write familiar things; to your hundred add a score.'

My friend, they would bestow
  Fame for a shadow-show,
And they would pay with praise for things dead as last year's
    leaves.
  But I look where the parrot, stilled,
  Hangs a head with rumours filled,
And I watch where my falcon turns her brooding and baleful
    eyes!

Come to my shoulder! Sit!
  To the bone be your talons knit!
I have sworn my friends shall have no parrot-speech from me;
  Who reads the verse I write
  Shall know the falcon's flight,
The vision single and sure, the conquest of air and sun!

Is there aught else worthy to weave within your banners' folds?
Is there aught else worthy to grave on the blades of your naked
   swords?"

Saadi, the Poet, stood up and he put forth his living words;
His songs were the hurtling of spears, and his figures the flashing
   of swords!
With hearts dilated the tribe saw the creature of Saadi's mind:
It was like to the horse of a king—a creature of fire and of wind!

Umimah, my loved one, was by me; without love did these eyes
   see my fawn,
And if fire there were in her being, for me its splendour was
   gone:
When the sun storms up on the tent it makes waste the fire of
   the grass:
It was thus with my loved one's beauty—the splendour of song
   made it pass!

The desert, the march, and the onset—these, and these only avail;
Hands hard with the handling of spear-shafts, brows white with
   the press of the mail!
And as for the kisses of women—these are honey, the poet sings,
But the honey of kisses, beloved—it is lime for the spirit's wings!

Ye know not why God hath joined the horse-fly unto the horse,
Nor why the generous steed should be yoked with the poisonous
   fly:
Lest the steed should sink into ease and lose his fervour of limb,
God hath bestowed on him this—a lustful and venomous bride!

Never supine lie they, the steeds of our folk, to the sting,
Praying for deadness of nerve with wounds the shame of the
    sun:
They strive, but they strive for this—the fullness of passionate
    nerve;
They pant, but they pant for this—the speed that outstrips the
    pain!

Sons of the Dust, ye have stung—there is darkness upon my soul!
Sons of the Dust, ye have stung—yea, stung to the roots of my
    heart!
But I have said in my breast—the birth succeeds to the pang,
And, Sons of the Dust, behold—your malice becomes my song!

"I Shall Not Die for Thee"

O WOMAN, shapely as the swan,
On your account I shall not die:
The men you've slain—a trivial clan—
Were less than I.

I ask me shall I die for these—
For blossom teeth and scarlet lips?
And shall that delicate swan-shape
Bring me eclipse?

Well-shaped the breasts and smooth the skin,
The cheeks are fair, the tresses free—
And yet I shall not suffer death,
God over me!

Those even brows, that hair like gold,
Those languorous tones, that virgin way,
The flowing limbs, the rounded heel
Slight men betray!

Thy spirit keen through radiant mien,
Thy shining throat and smiling eye,
Thy little palm, thy side like foam—
I cannot die!

O woman, shapely as the swan,
In a cunning house hard-reared was I:
O bosom white, O well-shaped palm,
I shall not die!

An Idyll

You stay for a while beside me with your beauty young and
　　rare,
Though your light limbs are as limber as the foal's that follows
　　the mare;
Brow fair and young and tender where thought has scarce begun,
Hair bright as the breast of the eagle when he strains up to the
　　sun!

In the space of a broken castle I found you on a day
When the call of the new-come cuckoo went with me all the
　　way,
You stood by un-mortised stones that were rough and black with
　　age,
The fawn beloved of the hunter in the panther's broken cage!

And we went down together by paths your childhood knew,
Remote you went beside me like the spirit of the dew,
Hard were the hedgerows still, sloe-bloom was their scanty
　　dower,
You slipped it within your bosom, the bloom that scarce is
　　flower!

And now you stay beside me with your beauty young and rare,
Though your light limbs are as limber as the foal's that follows
　　the mare,
Brow fair and young and tender where thought has scarce
　　begun,
Hair bright as the breast of the eagle when he strains up to the
　　sun!

Legend

THERE is an hour, they say,
On which your dream has power:
Then all you wish for comes,
As comes the lost field-bird
Down to the island-lights;
There is an hour, they say,
That's woven with your wish:
In dawn, or dayli' gone,
In mirk-dark, or at noon,
In hush or hum of day,
May be that secret hour.

A herd-boy in the rain
Who looked o'er stony fields;
A young man in a street,
When fife and drum went by,
Making the sunlight shrill;
A girl in a lane,
When the long June twilight
Made friendly far-off things,
Had watch upon the hour:
The dooms they met are in
The song my grand-dam sings.

Men on Islands

CAN it be that never more
Men will grow on Islands?
Ithaka and Eriskey,
Iceland and Tahiti!
Must the engines he has forged
Raven so for spaces
That the Islands dwindle down,
Dwindle down!—
Pots that shelve the tap-root's growth?
Must it be that never more
Men will flower on Islands?
Crete and Corsica, Mitylene,
Aran and Iona!

Branding the Foals

WHY do I look for fire to brand these foals?
What do I need, when all within is fire?
And lo, she comes, carrying the lighted coals
And branding-tool—she who is my desire!
What need have I for what is in her hands,
If I lay hand upon a hide it brands,
And grass, and trees, and shadows, all are fire!

Imitation of a Welsh Poem

AND that was when the chevaldour
Through the whole of night
Sang, for the moon of mid-July
Made the hillside bright.

Morfydd to David ap Gwillam spoke
When the song they did not hear,
"Something is stirring in the fern,
A living thing comes near."

'Twas not the wolf, 'twas not the deer
That came with pause and bound;
A creature stood above the pair—
Ap Gwillam's Irish hound—

And knew them then, and knew them there
Where the pine branches wave,
As close beside, as deep in earth,
As lone as in a grave!

To a Poet

BELOW there are white-faced throngs,
Their march is a tide coming nigher;
Below there are white-faced throngs,
Their faith is a banner flung higher;
Below there are white-faced throngs,
White swords they have yet, but red songs;
Place and lot they have lost—hear you not?
For a dream you once dreamed and forgot!

First East to West Atlantic Flyers

I

A SOLDIER, not of Fortune, but of some
Idea laboured by philosophers:
A soldier always, though there's monk in him,
And poet also: watch how he salutes
The anthem, or the ensign, or the line
Of marching men: his hand upraised, his eyes
Salute a drill, salute a chivalry:
Frederick of Prussia, Frederick Barbaross!

II

Something that's like the fabulous content
In whales or hippopotami is in him,
This small-eyed man of ample girth who stands
Square, a steersman! Vision must become
Readiness, wakefulness, and unfailing craft
To burst through longitudes, to beat the winds,
And fog and squalls make light of! This is he
Who fronts a course the arc-Atlantic wide!

III

January and gamey, like a lad that's in
A ballad that they sing in Kerry fairs,
One joins himself unto the two are here,
And he is of the breed of those who were
Soldiers of fortune born, who were wont
To put all skill and spirit in a charge—
The men who followed where the Wild Geese went:
Fortune still counts, and with them she will be!

The Wayfarer

I. THE TREES

THERE is no glory of the sunset here!
Heavy the clouds upon the darkening road,
And heavy, too, the wind upon the trees!
The trees sway, making moan
Continuous, like breaking seas.
O impotent, bare things,
You give at last the very cry of earth!
I walk this darkening road in solemn mood:
Within deep hell came Dante to a wood—
Like him I marvel at the crying trees!

II. THE STAR

A mighty star anear has drawn and now
Is vibrant on the air—

The half-divested, trembling trees of his
Bright presence are aware—

Below within the stream I him behold
Between the marge and main—

My bone and flesh, what dust they'll be when he,
That star, dips here again!

III. THE CAPTIVE ARCHER

To-morrow I will bend the bow:
My soul shall have her mark again,
My bosom feel the archer's strain.
No longer pacing to and fro
With idle hands and listless brain:

As goes the arrow, forth I go.
My soul shall have her mark again,
My bosom feel the archer's strain.
To-morrow I will bend the bow.

IV. TRIUMPHATORS

The drivers in the sunset race
Their coal-carts over cobble-stones—
Not draymen but triumphators:
Their bags are left with Smith and Jones,
They let the horses take their stride,
Which toss their forelocks in their pride.

Not blue nor green these factions wear
Which make career o'er Dublin stones;
But Pluto his own livery
Is what each whip-carrier owns.
The Cæsar of the cab-rank, I
Salute the triumph speeding by.

In the Carolina Woods

HERE you should lie, ye Kings of eld,
Barbarossa, Boabdil,
And Czar Lazar and Charlemagne,
Arthur, Gaelic Finn—
Here where the muffling Spanish mosses
Forests with forests fill!

Not in a cavern where the winds
Trample with battle-call,
But in these woods where branch and branch
From tree and tree let fall—
Not moss, but grey and cobweb beards,
Kings' cabalistic beards!

Here should you sleep your cycles out,
Ye Kings with hoary beards!

Hawaii

I

Not in a grove where each tree loses its presence, not singly, do Lehua trees grow; they are Lehua trees only when they grow as I saw them growing at Kapaho, on Hawaii.

When I had seen them before they were mingled with other trees, or they grew singly, a tree here and a tree there: looking upon them I had marvelled that the poets of Hawaii had emblemed their warriors as Lehua trees.

But in Kapaho, on Hawaii, they stand upon lava rock and upon lava crust; some like mighty champions, like Kamehameha, like Umi, stand upon high places, upon mounds and rocks of lava. All stand in ranks as if all the warriors of the Eight Islands stood spear-ready upon that lava waste.

With branches from the ground they grow. From top to bottom the blossoms show themselves—not blossoms but the precious ornaments the warrior decks himself with.

The blossoms show themselves amongst the leaves; they are like scarlet birds, the lost i-i-wi birds, come back to hide and show themselves in the trees beloved of Hiiaka.

They stand upon the lava waste, upon black rocks and amongst black shingles, rank upon rank they grow, like warriors standing erect in the red glow of the volcano.

I saw your lava-mounting trees, and I marvelled no more that your poets had emblemed your warriors as Lehua trees. . . .

They have departed, the warriors whom these trees emblemed. Honey for the birds of heaven, wreaths of red for girls to deck their lovers with—these your Lehua trees still bring out of your fire-formed rock, Hawaii.

II

I call on you, beloved—
Breast so cold, so cold!
Oh, so cold, I have to say
I ku anu e!

How very cold the wind is,
How very cold the dew—
Bodies all a-shiver say
I ku anu e!

What if this we do
Against wind, cold, and dew—
Arms put round each other?
Just so that we need not say
I ku anu e!

III

From afar it has come, that long-rolling wave; from Tahiti it has come; long has it been coming, that wide-sweeping wave; since the time of Wakea it has been on the way.

Now it plumes, now it ruffles itself. Stand upon your surf-board with the sun to lead you on! Stand! Gird your loin-cloth! The wave rolls and swells higher, the wave that will not break bears you along.

From afar it has come, that long-rolling wave; long has it been coming, that wide-sweeping wave. And now it bears you towards us, upright upon your board.

The wave-ridden waves dash upon the island; the deep-sea coral is swept in-shore; the long-rolling wave, the wide-sweeping wave comes on.

Glossy is your skin and undrenched; the wave-feathers fan the triumphing surf-rider; with the speed of the white tropic-bird you come to us.

We have seen the surf at Puna; we have seen a triumphing surf-rider: Na-i-he is his name.

IV

The old back-turning world has passed him by,
The world that left Columbus in his chains,
And Belisarius begging from his curb,
And Clown Grimaldi weeping lonely tears!
But he knew not these names that mean to us
Fortune's wheel turned: his Columbus sailed
Up the Pacific in canoes were hollowed
In Hawaiki with the greenstone axes,
In Hawaiki in the old, lost days.

I found him once, old game-cock on the roost,
Watching with shuttered eye, and had him take me
Where Laka was not—
Laka the goddess of the green-branched altar,
Where he was master of a dance was merely
Bellies like millstones turning; yet he sat there

Like some great virtuoso who's once more
Before his audience; he wore the ilima wreath,
And from the ipu, from the gourd he rattled,
Came sounds as strange as echoes—
Came sounds like echoes from Hawaiian caves. . . .
. . . Far, far within the dance is for the King,
The wreaths are smelling like an isle of flowers,
And like an isle of sea-birds rising up,
The dancers move, and he is there, the Master!

The crocus-yellow ilima grows beside
His grave: 'tis where canoes once sailed
For Bolotua and the Southern Seas;
His house is overgrown—that quiet house
That had an old man sleeping on its mats.

V

The sign is given; mighty the sign: *Tapu!*
All murmurs now, speech, voice,
Subdue: inviolable let evening be.

Inviolable and consecrate:
Edgeways and staggering descends
The sun; rain vanishes;
A bonus of bright light comes back.
Hawaii keeps the ordinance: *Tapu!*
Even far Tahiti now is still, perhaps.

The Island's shelter-giving houses stand;
The Chief withdraws, the sacred cup is his;
The mothers call on Kuhe as they give
Their babes to sleep. O early slumber

Of the heavenly company thou art indeed!
O Ku, O Lono, O Kane, they are yours
The evening hours (subdue
All murmurs now, speech, voice;
Inviolate let evening be).

It is evening; it is hallowed for being that:
Let tumult die within us all: *Tapu!*
The spies of heaven, the stars return: *Tapu!*
And peaceful heaven covers peaceful earth.

CREATURES

TO

LLEWELYN POWYS

David Ap Gwillan at the Mass of the Birds

The Thrush, the Lark, and, chief, the Nightingale,
With one small bird whose name I do not ken,
Offered a Mass; the little bird was clerk,
At intervals he struck his silver bell.
The stars above that were but whitened then
The candles were; the altar was a stone;
Myself was there, with meet observances
Hearing the Mass the birds said in the dell.

It was the Lark who sang in dark's decrease
Kyrie Eleison; then the Nightingale
The Consecration chanted solemnly.
(The silver bell was rung for him in chief.)
And then the Thrush, the dweller in the vale,
Orate Fratres sang—how near, how clear!
The Thrush it was who, as the sun appeared,
Held up the Monstrance, a dew-circled leaf!

Jackdaw

ALOOF from his tribe
On the elm-tree's top,
A jackdaw perched
A hand-reach up.

Silent he sat
On the branch, nor stirred,
And I saw in him
A changeling bird.

Grass was worn
Round pots and a pan,
A flea-bitten horse,
And a tilted van,

Where tinker's or gypsy's
Brats at play
Made vagrant's game of
Some citizen's way.

I watched the daw
On the branch, beguiled:
I saw a vagrant
From the wild.

The entail broken
What had he?
The humour of one
Out of his degree.

The franchise of one
Without kith or kind,

And only the pauper's
Single mind!

The daws on the elms
Kept tribal speech,
And he perched there,
Within a hand's reach—

He flew; his flight
Neither high nor wide
Was a vagabond's
To a seedman's stride.

A dog on the ground
Was rubbing for fleas;
Rags were there—
He fluttered to these:

Held a bright rag up
Like a banner won,
And went and hid it
Behind a stone!

Crows

THEN, suddenly, I was aware indeed
Of what he said, and was revolving it:
How, in the night, crows often take to wing,
Rising from off the tree-tops in Drumbarr,
And flying on: I pictured what he told.

The crows that shake the night-damp off their wings
Upon the stones out yonder in the fields,
The first live things that we see in the mornings;
The crows that march across the fields, that sit
Upon the ash-trees' branches, that fly home
And crowd the elm-tops over in Drumbarr;
The crows we look on at all hours of light,
Growing, and full, and going—these black beings have
Another lifetime!

Crows flying in the dark—
Blackness in darkness flying; beings unseen
Except by eyes that are like to their own
Trespassers' eyes!

And you, old man, with eyes so quick and sharp,
Who've told me of the crows, my fosterer;
And you, old woman, upon whose lap I've lain
When I was taken from my mother's lap;
And you, young girl, with looks that have come down
From forefathers, my kin—ye have another life—
I've glimpsed it, I becoming trespasser—
Blackness in darkness flying like the crows!

Otters

I'll be an otter, and I'll let you swim
A mate beside me; we will venture down
A deep, full river when the sky above
Is shut of the sun; spoilers are we;
Thick-coated; no dog's tooth can bite at our veins—
With ears and eyes of poachers; deep-earthed ones
Turned hunters: let him slip past,
The little vole, my teeth are on an edge
For the King-fish of the River!

I hold him up—
The glittering salmon that smells of the sea:
I hold him up and whistle!

Now we go
Back to our earth; we will tear and eat
Sea-smelling salmon: you will tell the cubs
I am the Booty-bringer: I am the Lord
Of the River—the deep, dark, full, and flowing River!

Asses

"I KNOW where I'd get
An ass that would do,
If I had the money—
A pound or two."

Said a ragged man
To my uncle one day;
He got the money
And went on his way.

And after that time
In market or fair
I'd look at the asses
That might be there.

And wonder what kind
Of an ass would do
For a ragged man
With a pound or two.

O the black and roan horses the street would fill,
Their manes and tails streaming, and they standing still,

And their owners, the men of estate, would be there,
Refusing gold guineas for a colt or a mare.

And one, maybe, riding up and down like a squire
So that buyers from Dublin might see and admire

The hunter or racer come to be sold
And be willing and ready to pay out their gold.

With men slouching beside them and buyers not near
It's no wonder the asses held down head and ear.

They had been sold or in by-ways bought
For a few half-crowns tied up in a knot,

And no one so poor as to buy one might come
To that fair that had horses so well prized at home!

     And then it fell out
     That at Arva or Scrabbey,
     At some down-county fair,
     Or Mohill or Abbey,

     On two asses I happened—
     Without duress or dole
     They were there in the market,
     A dam and her foal.

     And the owner, a woman,
     Did not slouch or stand,
     But in her cart sitting
     Was as grand as the grand;

     Like a queen out of Connacht
     From her toe to her tip,
     Like proud Grania Uaile
     On the deck of her ship.

     And her hair—'twas a mane:
     The blackberries growing
     Out of the hedge-rows
     Have the sheen it was showing.

There kind was with kind
Like the flowers in the grasses
If the owner was fine,
As fine were her asses.

White, white was the mother
As a dusty white road;
Black on back and on shoulders
The cross-marking showed.

She was tall—she could carry
A youth stout of limb,
Or bear down from her mountain
The bride decked for him!

Such was the mother—
The foal's hide was brown,
All fleecy and curly,
And soft like bog-down;

And it nuzzled its mother,
Its head to her knee,
And blue were its eyes
Like the pools of the sea!

Then I thought all the silver
My uncle could draw
Might not pay for the creatures
That that day I saw;

And I thought that old Damer,
Who had troughs made of gold,
Could not pay for the asses,
The young and the old.

And I think of them still
When I see on the roads
Asses unyoked,
And asses with loads;

One running and trotting,
With harness loose,
And a man striking and hitting
Where his stick has use;

And one with a hide
Like a patched-on sack
And two creels of turf
Upon its back;

And one in the market,
Meek and brown,
Its head to the cart-shafts
That are down;

Eating its forage—
A wisp of hay;
In the dust of the highway
Munching away;

Unmarked in the market
As might be a mouse
Behind a low stool
In a quiet house—

Then I think of the pair
Horses might not surpass—
The dam and her foal,
The white ass and brown ass.

Pigeons

I

ODALISQUES, odalisques,
Treading the pavement
With feet pomegranate-stained:
We bartered for, bought you
Back in the years—
Ah, then we knew you,
Odalisques, odalisques,
Treading the pavement
With feet pomegranate-stained!

Queens of the air—
Aithra, Iole,
Eos and Auge,
Taking new beauty
From the sun's evening brightness,
Gyring in light
As nymphs play in waters—
Aithra, Iole,
Eos and Auge!

Then down on our doorsteps,
Gretchen and Dora. . . .

II

Pigeons that have flown down from the courts behind the
orchards! Pigeons that run along the beach to take sand into your
crops! What contrast is between you, birds of a rare stock, and
the waves that know only the buccaneer sea-gulls and the sand-

marten emigrants! And what contrast is between your momentary wildness here and your graces in the courtyards beyond the orchards!

You rise up and fly out five wave lengths from the beach. And now a strange element is under you—the green, tumbling, untried sea. With that half-remembered element below you, you think, maybe, of rocky breeding-places and strong mates. Bravely you hang above the untried, alluring sea—just five wave-lengths out!

You remind us of the ladies who came down to the gypsy carts that were on the beach yesterday, and swore they would take to the gypsy ways!

And now you run along by the waves, taking more grains of sand into your crops!

A wave-break startles you. You take to your wings again. Now you see the dove-cotes beyond the orchards, and you fly towards them.

And all night long you will hear the sea breaking, and you will dream, maybe, in the dove-cotes, of strong mates and rocky breeding places.

At dawn you will fly down to the beach again, run along the hard sand, take grains into your crops, and fly five wave-lengths from the beach.

The sand-martens will have left their holes, and you will see them gathered in flocks on the sand-heights, the dusky gypsies.

And you will not notice when they have departed, going without after-thoughts, going over that green, alluring element, the sea.

Pigeons that run along the beach, taking sand into your crops!

Swallow

He knows Queen Lab, her isle,
And black, enormous Kaf,
The Swallow, and "Allah"
          He cries

As into Giaour lands
With Dervish faith and rite,
Hueless, a Saracen,
          He flies.

Like scimitars his wings,
And, all unluminous,
Black, like a genie's thought,
          His eyes.

Crane

I KNOW you, Crane:
I, too, have waited,
Waited until my heart
Melted to little pools around my feet!

Comer in the morning ere the crows,
Shunner,
Searcher—
Something find for me!
The pennies that were laid upon the eyes
Of old, wise men I knew.

The Little Fox

THAT sidling creature is a little Fox:
Like other canine he is leashed and led;
He goes upon the sidewalk; houses tower;
Men trample; horses rear; he drags his leash.

Did not I
Once know a lad from Irrus where they leave
Mittens for foxes; where they invite
A fox to a child's christening; where they have
Foxes as gossips to their boys and girls?

Would that a lad from Irrus now was here
To tell his gossip that a human creature
Has heart for him, and fain would cover up
His bowels of dread, and find some way to bring
His rainy hills around him, the soft grass,
Darkness of ragged hedges, and his earth—
The black, damp earth under the roots of trees!
Would that a lad from Irrus now was here
Where houses tower and where horses rear!

Wild Ass

THE Wild Ass lounges, legs struck out
In vagrom unconcern:
The tombs of Achaemenian kings
Are for those hooves to spurn.

And all of rugged Tartary
Lies with him on the ground,
The Tartary that knows no awe,
That has nor ban nor bound.

The wild horse from the herd is plucked
To bear a saddle's weight;
The boar is one keeps covert, and
The wolf runs with a mate.

But he's the solitary of space,
Curbless and unbeguiled;
The only being that bears a heart
Not recreant to the wild.

Monkeys

Two little creatures
With faces the size of
A pair of pennies
Are clasping each other.
"Ah, do not leave me,"
One says to the other,
In the high monkey-
Cage in the beast-shop.

There are no people
To gape at them now,
For people are loth to
Peer in the dimness;
Have they not builded
Streets and playhouses,
Sky-signs and bars,
To lose the loneliness
Shaking the hearts
Of the two little Monkeys?

Yes. But who watches
The penny-small faces
Can hear the voices:
"Ah, do not leave me;
Suck I will give you,
Warmth and clasping,
And if you slip from
This beam I can never
Find you again."

Dim is the evening,
And chill is the weather;

There, drawn from their coloured
Hemisphere,
The apes lilliputian
With faces the size of
A pair of pennies,
And voices as low as
The flow of my blood.

Bison

How great a front is thine—
A lake of majesty!
Assyria knew the sign—
The god-incarnate king!

A lake of majesty—
The lion's drowns in it!
And thy placidity—
A moon within that lake!

As if thou still dost own
A world, thou takest breath—
Earth-shape and strength of stone,
A Titan-sultan's child!

Snake

But, Snake, you must not come where we abide,
For you would tempt us; we should hear you say:

"Oh, somewhere was a world was cold and spare,
And voiceless; somewhere was a Being was not

Engrossed with substance, with no fervencies
Of love and hatred, and he made me, Snake!

The wise Elohim, they who made the rest
Of Creatures, made them all-too manifold—

Mortised and rampired, jointed, vascular;
And I was put an alien in their world,

All head, all spine, all limb, all loin,
Swift as a bird and single as a fish."

Above you fruits unglanced at bend and glow,
And, bare and voiceless, you do tempt us, Snake!

Aquarium Fish

MOULD-COLOURED like the leaf long fallen from
The autumn branch, he rises now, the Fish.
The cold eyes of the gannets see their rock:
He has No-whither. Who was it marked
Earth from the waters? Who
Divided space into such lines for us,
Giving men To and Fro, not Up and Down?
This dweller in the ancient element
Knows Space's cross-road. Who
Closed up the Depth to us? He rises now
Mould-coloured like the leaf long fallen from
The autumn branch, with eyes that are like lamps
Magicians fill with oils from dead men ta'en,
Most rootless of all beings, the Fish.

Night-Fliers

THE birds that soar break space
Like heavy bodies hurled!
Not so the birds of night—
They move as in a sphere
On which they touch always—
How patterned their flight!
The owl, the whippoorwill!

And like volcano's ash
His plumes—all cinderous
Black mirrors are his eyes
(The owl's). They'll fill with light
What time will come the cries
As from tongues taut with dews
(The whippoorwill's). What sounds
Are in their day-lost world,
What motions and what hues!

Bat

In broad daylight
He should not be:
Yet toward and froward,
Froward and toward
He weaves a flight.
Who will guide him back to his cave,
A little Bat astray,
Where he'll rest on the breast of night,
Away from day's bright miscreation?
The linnet throbs through the air,
The magpie coquettes with day,
The rook caws "Time to be gone,"
And travels on;
While toward and froward,
Froward and toward,
The Bat . . . a fathom
Of flight . . . weaves.

Bird of Paradise

WITH sapphire for her crown,
And with the Libyan wine
For lustre of her eyes;
With azure for her feet
(It is her henna stain);
Then iris for her vest,
Rose, ebony, and flame,
She lives a thing enthralled,
In forests that are old,
As old as is the Moon.

Humming-Bird

Up from the navel of the world,
Where Cuzco has her founts of fire,
The passer of the Gulf he comes.

He lives in air, a bird of fire,
Charted by flowers still he comes
Through spaces that are half the world.

With glows of suns and seas he comes;
A life within our shadowed world
That's bloom, and gem, and kiss of fire!

The Resplendent Quetzal-Bird

OTHERS have divers paints and enamels,
Lavish and bright on breast and wing feathers:
You, Guatemalan, have sunken all colours
Into glory of greenness!

There may be palms as greenly resplendent,
Palms by the Fountain of Youth in Anahuac—
Such greens there may be on sea-sunken bronzes—
The Gates of Callao!

There may be words in rituals spoken
To Quetzalcoatl who makes verdure through rain-flow—
Words like the gash made by knives of obsidian—
To tell of such greenness!

Vultures

Foul-feathered and scald-necked,
They sit in evil state;
Raw marks upon their breasts
As on men's wearing chains.

Impure, though they may plunge
Into the morning's springs,
And spirit-dulled, though they
Command the heaven's heights.

Angels of foulness, ye,
So fierce against the dead!
Sloth on your muffled wings,
And speed within your eyes!

Hornets

How strangely like a churchyard skull
The thing that's there amongst the leaves!

—A Hornets' nest; but stir the branch
And they'll be round your head and ears!

So wary and so weaponéd,
How do they not possess the wold?

—Their lives a watch, their act a doom,
Of their own terrors they must die!

Livid, uneyed, articulate,
How like a skull their nest they make!

Plovers

THE Plovers fly and cry around,
Unguided, nestless, without bourn,
Wandering and impetuous,
Turning and flying to return.

These wild birds seen on Ireland's ground
I name upon Hawaiian beaches—
Estrayents, they, of all lands' ends,
They have the oceans for their reaches.

My thoughts are like the Plovers' flight,
Unguided, nestless, without bourn,
Wandering and impetuous,
Turning and flying to return.

Condors

I. CONDORS FLYING

We watched the Condors winging towards the Moon,
A Moon that glimmered in the blue daylight;
Around us were the Andes, and beyond
Andes, the Ocean, empty like the Moon.
I heard you speak in Atahualpa's tongue:
Then distances grew present; all the range
Of Condors' wings between my thought, your thought:
As though they had transcended need for wings,
We watched the Condors winging towards the Moon.

II. CONDORS IN THE JARDIN DES PLANTES

To sink into the depths we need take weights—
Put on such armour as our divers use;
To rise above the fathomed we must bear
Weights, and you are weighted for emprise
Of rising to where flows the thinnest air,
And here beneath our towers you roost and run,
And trail your wings. I think I know your pain,
Your pain and weariness!
Like divers are ye that perpetually,
Plated in metal, make circuit about
Where some sidereal gesture has withdrawn
The tides, the main—
Condors with shuttered, iron-heavy wings!

OLD PASTURES

Dublin Roads

When you were a lad that lacked a trade,
Oh, many's the thing you'd see on the way
From Kill-o'-the-Grange to Ballybrack,
And from Cabinteely down into Bray,
When you walked these roads the whole of a day.

High walls there would be to the left and right,
With ivies growing across the top,
And a briary ditch on the other side,
And a place where a quiet goat might crop,
And a wayside bench where a man could stop.

A hen that had found a thing in her sleep,
One would think, the way she went craw-craw-cree,
You would hear as you sat on the bench was there,
And a cock that thought he crew mightily,
And all the stir of the world would be

A cart that went creaking along the road,
And another cart that kept coming a-near;
A man breaking stones; for bits of the day
One stroke and another would come to you clear,
And then no more from that stone-breaker.

And his day went by as the clouds went by,
As hammer in hand he sat alone,
Breaking the mendings of the road;
The dazzles up from the stones were thrown
When, after the rain, the sun down-shone.

And you'd leave him there, that stone-breaker,
And you'd wonder who came to see what was done

By him in a day, or a month, or a week:
He broke a stone and another one,
And you left him there and you travelled on.

A quiet road! You would get to know
The briars and stones along by the way;
A dozen times you'd see last year's nest;
A peacock's cry, a pigeon astray
Would be marks enough to set on a day;

Or the basket-carriers you would meet—
A man and a woman—they were a pair!
The woman going beside his heel:
A straight-walking man with a streak of him bare,
And eyes that would give you a crafty stare.

Coming down from the hills they'd have ferns to sell,
Going up from the strand they'd have cockles in stock:
Sand in their baskets from the sea,
Or clay that was stripped from a hillside rock—
A pair that had often stood in the dock!

Or a man that played on a tin-whistle:
He looked as he'd taken a scarecrow's rig;
Playing and playing as though his mind
Could do nothing else but go to a jig,
And no one around him, little or big.

And you'd meet no man else until you came
Where you could look down upon the sedge,
And watch the Dargle water flow,
And men smoke pipes on the bridge's ledge,
While a robin sang by the haws in a hedge.

Or no bird sang, and the bird-catchers
Would have talk enough for a battle gained,
When they came from the field and stood by the bridge,
Taking shelter beside it while it rained,
While the bird new-caught huddled and strained

In this cage or that, a linnet or finch,
And the points it had were declared and surmised:
And this one's tail was spread out, and there
Two little half-moons, the marks that were prized;
And you looked well on the bird assized.

Then men would go by with a rick of hay
Piled on a cart; with them you would be
Walking beside the piled-up load:
It would seem as it left the horses free,
They went with such stride and so heartily—

And so you'll go back along the road.

Laburnums

Over old walls the Laburnums
            hang cones of fire;
Laburnums that grow out of old
            mould in old gardens:

Old maids and old men who have savings or pensions have
Shuttered themselves in the pales of old gardens.

The gardens grow wild; out of their mould the Laburnums
Draw cones of fire.

And we, who've no lindens, no palms, no cedars of Lebanon,
Rejoice you have gardens with mould, old men and old maids:

The bare and the dusty streets have now the Laburnums,
Have now cones of fire!

Lilac Blossoms

WE mark the playing-time of sun and rain,
Until the rain too heavily upon us
Leans, and the sun stamps down upon our lustres,
And then our trees stand in their greennesses
No different from the privets in the hedges,
And we who made a pleasaunce at the door-step,
And, whether by the ash-heap or the spring-well
Growing, were ever fresh and ever radiant,
And fragrant more than grass is—
We, we are gone without a word that praised us—
You did not know how short the playing-time!

Fuchsia Hedges in Connacht

I THINK some saint of Eirinn wandering far
Found you and brought you here—
Demoiselles!
For so I greet you in this alien air!

And like those maidens who were only known
In their own land as daughters of the King,
Children of Charlemagne—
You have, by following that pilgrim-saint,
Become high vot'resses—
You have made your palace—beauty dedicate,
And your pomp serviceable:
You stand beside our folds!

I think you came from some old Roman land—
Most alien, but most Catholic are you:
Your purple is the purple that enfolds,
In Passion Week, the Shrine,
Your scarlet is the scarlet of the wounds:
You bring before our walls, before our doors
Lamps of the Sanctuary;
And in this stony place
The time the robin sings,
Through your bells rings the Angelus!

At Cashel

Above me stand, worn from their ancient use,
The King's, the Bishop's, and the Warrior's house,
Quiet as folds upon a grassy knoll:
Stark-grey they stand, wall joined to ancient wall,
Chapel, and Castle, and Cathedral.

It is not they are old, but stone by stone
Into another lifetime they have grown,
The life of memories an old man has:
They dream upon what things have come to pass,
And know that stones grow friendly with the grass.

The name has crumbled—Cashel that has come
From conqueror-challenging Castellum—
Walls in a name! No citadel is here,
Now as a fane the empty walls uprear
Where green and greener grass spreads far and near!

Verses for Alfeo Faggi's
Stations of the Cross

I

HERE Pilate's Court is:
None may clatter nor call
Where the Wolf giving suck
To the Twins glares on all
"Strip Him and scourge Him
Till flesh shows the blood,
And afterwards nail Him
On cross of wood."

O Lord
Silence in us the condemning word!

II

Heaven witnesseth, but only in the heart
Is any aid:
"They know not what they do," and then on Him
The Cross is laid—
The Cross that's wide and long enough to bear
His flesh and bone:
A spectacle unto the crowded way,
The Man goes on.

The Father's will
May we know also, and may we fulfil!

III

Beneath the load
The knees quail;

The heart pants,
The joints fail;
Almost the bones break;
He faints, his breath being loss;
He sinks beneath the Cross!

                May we
Be mindful of this road to Calvary!

IV

Jesus His Mother meets:
She looks on Him and sees
The Saviour in Her Son:
The Angel's word comes back:
Within her heart she says,
"Unto me let this be done!"
Still is she full of grace.

                    By us, too, be it won
The grace that brings us revelation!

V

"If He should die upon the road
That were a turn of ill:
'Tis fixed the Crucifixion be
Upon that skull-shaped hill.
Ho, man who looks with pity on
The Man we take to death—
Bear you the Cross—I order it—
Until He wins back breath."

We take
Our hearts being moved, the Cross up for Thy sake!

VI

Down to her face His face He bends:
The helper she, the heartner:
His image in her cloth He leaves;
He leaves it, too, to all like her
Who serve within a little room,
But run to help outside the door,
Who mend and brighten needed things:
He leaves it to good hearts, the Poor!

May we, too, wait,
Like her, and help, and be compassionate!

VII

The Spirit is willing—aye,
But weak the flesh put on;
Deadly the Cross's weight;
He stumbles on a stone,
And lies upon the road,
Seeing His Body's blood.

May we
Forget not in these times that agony!

VIII

Heavy the Cross is:
He drags beneath its beam,

Yet, Women of Jerusalem,
Weep not for Him:
Weep for your children, rather,
For that they cannot see
The true Son of David,
The Saviour, shown ye.

O Lord,
Also to us say the revealing word!

IX

The skull-shaped hill is near:
The earth and heaven are bare
Of light, and sight, and sound;
He falls upon the ground,
Knowing that journey's end
Without one to befriend.

O Lord
Bring us to Life according to Thy word!

X

"Wouldst have me share this cloth,
Dividing it with sword?—
Nay, fellow, we will keep it whole,
But hearken to my word:
Behind the Cross the dice
We'll throw; who wins will get
What's high enough in price
To pay a tavern debt."

The vesture that makes one with Thee our soul,
May we keep whole!

XI

"This thong, I know, will last;
Draw out the arm and make it fast;
Through hand and board with strength
Drive the nail of mickle length.
Now, King of the Jews, in the sun,
Gape, for our work is done."

God send
That our labours have no evil end!

XII

The birds are flying home,
Now darkened is the sky,
And He hath given up
With that great bitter cry
The ghost, and on the Cross
(His Mother stays by it),
The title rightly His,
KING—is writ.

May we draw near
Considering in our hearts what Man is here!

XIII

Though pitiful it is to see
The wounds, the broken Body,

(The Body of Him that was
As fair as lily of the grass!)
Though the brow with thorns is riven,
And a spear through the side is driven,
It was all for our healing done,
Mother, by thy Son!

May we
This Body in its glory come to see!

XIV

Now in the tomb is laid
Who had neither house nor hall,
Who in the wide world walked,
And talked with one and all;
Who told the sparrow's worth,
The lily's praises said,
Who kept wakeful in the garden
Now in the tomb is laid.

His Spirit still doth move
On a new way of love!

L'ENVOI

Prince, by thine own darkened hour,
Live within me, heart and brain;
Let my hands not slip the rein!

Ah, how long ago the hour
Since a comrade rode with me:
Now, a moment, let me see

Thyself, lonely in the dark,
Perfect, without wound nor mark!

Breffne Caoine

Not as a woman of the English weeping over a lord of the
  English
Do I weep—
A cry that scarcely stirs the heart!
I lament as it is in my blood to lament—
Castle and stronghold are broken,
And the sovereign of the land beside the lake lies dead—
Mahon O'Reilly!
In his day the English were broken:
I weep beside Loch Sheelin and the day is long and grey!

On Two Sisters Whose Deaths Were Together

In woods remote, hid in the mountain hollows,
Doves there are that have a gentler beauty,
Doves that are marked as by a poet's image,
And hence are called Doves of the Wounded Heart.

And such ye were, and we could never learn the
Call that would bring you to our breasts, our hands!
And such ye were, and ye were aliens in our
Barnyard-world—Doves of the Wounded Heart!

You who were proud no storm had ever turned your
Flight, and you who were her cherished one—
May ye have found, hid in your mountain hollows,
Your wood remote, Doves of the Wounded Heart!

In Memory of John Butler Yeats

"To-night," you said, "to-night, all Ireland round
The curlews call." The dinner-talk went on,
And I knew what you heard and what you saw,
That left you for a little while withdrawn—
The lonely land, the lonely-crying birds!

Your words, your breath is gone!
O uncaught spirit, we'll remember you
By those remote and ever-flying birds
Adown the Shannon's reach, or crying through
The mist between Clew Bay and Dublin Bay!

The Rune-Master

ARCH-SCHOLAR they'll call you,
Kuno Mayer,
Who know the word
Behind the word—
The men of learning . . .
But who will tell them
Of the blackbird
That your heart held?

On an old thorn-tree
By an ancient rath
You heard him sing,
And with runes you charmed him
Till he stayed with you,
Giving clear song.

He sang o'er all
That Maravaun
Told King Guire;
And he told you how
Bran heard the singing
Of a lovely woman
And sailed for Faerie;
And of how slain princes
Kept tryst with women
Loved beyond
The pain of death,
In days when still
The boat of Mananaun
Bore towards Eirinn!

Arch-scholar they'll call you—
Nay, Rune-master!
You read in texts
Not words only,
But runes of old time;
And when you spoke them
A curlew cried
Over grass-waste Tara,
And a cuckoo called
From the height of Cashel,
And an eagle flew
From Emain Macha!

Ochone, ochone!
That we'll see no more
In the Eastern or
The Western World
Your great head over
The lectern bending,
Nor hear your lore
By a pleasant fireside.

But the runes you've read
Have given us more
Than the sword might win us:
May kind saints of Eirinn
Be beside you
Where birds on the Living
Tree sing the Hours!

Odysseus: In Memory of Arthur Griffith

You had the prose of logic and of scorn,
And words to sledge an iron argument,
And yet you could draw down the outland birds
To perch beside the ravens of your thought—
The dreams whereby a people challenges
Its dooms, its bounds. You were the one who knew
What sacred resistance is in men
That are almost broken; how, from resistance used,
A strength is born, a stormy, bright-eyed strength
Like Homer's Iris, messenger of the gods,
Coming before the ships the enemy
Has flung the fire upon. Our own, our native strength
You mustered up. But I will never say this,
Walking beside you, or looking on you,
With your strong brow, and chin was like a targe,
And eyes that were so kindly of us all.

And sorrow comes as on that August day,
With our ship cleaving through the seas for home,
And that news coming sparkling through the air,
That you were dead, and that we'd never see you
Looking upon the state that you had builded.

The news that came was like that weight of waters
Poured on our hopes! Our navies yet unbuilded,
Our city left inglorious on its site,
Our fields uncleared, and over
Our ancient house the ancient curse of war!
And could we pray, touching the island-homeland,
Other than this: "Odysseus, you who laboured
So long upon the barren outer sea;

Odysseus, Odysseus, you who made
The plan that drove the wasters from the house,
And bent the bow that none could bend but you:
Be with us still:
Your memory be the watcher in our house,
Your memory be the flame upon our hills."

Roger Casement

THEY have hanged Roger Casement to the tolling of a bell,
Ochone, och, ochone, ochone!
And their Smiths, and their Murrays, and their Cecils say it's well,
Ochone, och, ochone, ochone!
But there are outcast peoples to lift that spirit high,
Flayed men and breastless women who laboured fearfully,
And they will lift him, lift him, for the eyes of God to see,
And it's well, after all, Roger Casement!

They've ta'en his strangled body from the gallows to the pit,
Ochone, och, ochone, ochone!
And the flame that eats into it, the quicklime, brought to it,
Ochone, och, ochone, ochone!
To waste that noble stature, the grave and brightening face,
In which courtesy and kindliness had eminence of place,
But they—they'll die to dust which the wind will take a-pace,
While 'twas yours to die to fire, Roger Casement!

Before the Fair

"Lost," "lost," the beeves and the bullocks,
The cattle men sell and buy,
Crowded upon the fair green,
Low to the lightless sky.

"Live," "live," and "Here," "here," the blackbird
From the top of the bare ash-tree,
Over the acres whistles
With beak of yellow blee.

And climbing, turning, and climbing
His little stair of sound,
"Content," "content," from the low hedge
The redbreast sings in a round.

And I who hear that hedge-song
Will fare with all the rest,
With thoughts of lust and labour,
And bargain in my breast.

The bare hedge bright with rain-drops
That have not fallen down,
The golden-crowded whin-bush—
Nor know these things my own!

Ave Atque Vale

Thorough waters, thorough nations I have come
To lay last offerings at your low abode,
Brother, and to appeal
To ashes that were you.

Since that which none can check has borne you
From my regard, poor brother, these gifts take—
The tokens that are due
To ancient pieties;

But find them washed with tears, the many tears
A brother shed; and now I say Farewell—
Henceforth and for all time,
Hail, brother, and Farewell!

The Landing

THE great ship lantern-girdled,
The tender standing by;
The waning stars cloud-shrouded,
The land that we descry!

That pale land is our homeland,
And we are bound therefor;
On her lawns nor in her coppice
No birds as yet make stir.

But birds are flying round us,
The white birds of the sea—
It is the breeze of morning,
This that comes hummingly.

And like the talk that comes from
A room where a babe is born—
Such clearness and such mystery
Are in words said on the morn,

Where, like a nation cloven,
In two our ranks divide:
One half on the high ship's bulwark,
One half by the tender's side;

Where, like a people sundered,
Who yet have each other's hail,
Faces look down from the bulwarks,
And look up from the tender's rail;

And names are called and spoken—
"Nancy," "Mary," "Owen"!

"Good-bye, and keep your promise!"
"Farewell to you, my son!"

They are more spirit-stirring
Than any words that are
Remembered from the spokesmen
Of any avatar!

"Oh, all I had to tell you!"
"Ellen," "Michael," "Joan"—
"Good-bye, and God be with you!"
"And can it be you're gone!"

The great ship lantern-girdled,
Her engines thresh, immerse—
The great ship that had station
Takes motion for her course.

Her little course the tender,
Our little ship, goes on—
The stars they are fast waning,
But we'll land ere 'tis the dawn!

Green, greener grows the foreland
Across the slate-dark sea,
And I'll see faces, places
That have been dreams to me!

Notes

Page 16. "Queen Gormlai" is a translation of an Irish mediæval poem, not, however, of one of the eleven poems that are attributed to Queen Gormlai (Gormlaith). She was the wife of Niall Blackknee who was killed in battle with the Norse in 917, and her poems are lamentations for the death of her husband and for her own state of dependence in a Leinster household away from her husband's Ulster kingdom.

Page 63. In "Girls Spinning" the refrains are nonsense lines; the spinners used them to keep the song going while questions and answers were being improvised.

Page 88. "A Man Bereaved" is a translation of a Scots Gaelic poem.

Page 94. "The Lannan Shee" in the first line of "Spinning Songs" is the Fairy Mistress. The name in the second line should be pronounced according to Gaelic usage—"Breean" so as to get the assonance with "Shee."

Page 101. "Garadh." This title is from the name of a man in the Finn Saga who laments the passing of his youth. The name is pronounced "Gara."

Page 106. "Sojourning and Wandering." The autumn piece is a translation of an Irish mediæval poem, and the spring piece translates the opening of a well-known eighteenth-century poem —Raftery's "County Mayo."

Pages 108, 109. "Shall I go bound and You go free?" and "She moved through the Fair," are restorations of Irish traditional songs of which one or two lines were in existence; they were written for traditional music collected by Herbert Hughes and published with the words given here in one of his collections.

Page 115. "An Drinaun Donn" is a translation of a famous song which is given in Dr. Douglas Hyde's "Love Songs of

Connacht." The title means "The blossom of the blackthorn," but there is nothing in the song that would suggest that title.

Page 120. "A Poor Scholar of the 'Forties." The scholar belonged to the time when O'Connell was carrying on an agitation for the Repeal of the Union between Ireland and Great Britain and when the Young Ireland group were trying to prepare the way for an insurrection. "Gall" in Irish means "Foreigner"—as opposed to "Gael" it has something of the sense of "barbarian."

Page 134. " 'I shall not die for thee' " is a translation from the Irish; it, too, is given in that collection of folk-poetry of the West of Ireland to which I owe a great debt—"The Love Songs of Connacht"—it is not, however, a folk poem.

Page 138. "Branding the Foals" is a reminiscence of a Latin epigram.

Page 141. "First East to West Atlantic Flyers" was written about the German-Irish airmen who were the first to cross the Atlantic from east to west—Baron von Hühnefeld, Captain Kohl and Major Fitzmaurice.

Page 145. "Hawaii." The heroic character and history of the Kanaka-Maori people rather than their soft charm appealed to me, and so I put first in this little collection a piece about the emblem of their warriors—the lehua blossom. This imitates but does not translate an Hawaiian poem. The second piece is a translation—it is a little popular song evidently made under European influence—the refrain means "from the cold." The third is a translation—it is *mele inoa* or name-song, belonging to a type which is made to introduce a character and name. The fifth is a translation of the famous "Mele Ahiahi" or Evening Song: it should be noted that the word *tapu* has a more extended meaning than the one we have imposed on it in "taboo"—it means consecrated to or belonging to the gods.

Page 194. The Stations of the Cross for which these verses

were written are in bronze; they are in St. Thomas's Church, Chicago.

, Page 200. "Breffne Caoine." The period of this lament would be the fifteenth century. The Breffne that was the O'Reilly territory is the modern county Cavan—"The Brenny" of the English historians.

Page 203. The dialogue between Guire and Maravaun, "King and Hermit," was translated by Kuno Meyer, as was "The Voyage of Bran." The other translation by this scholar referred to in the lament is "The tryst after Death" given in his "Ancient Irish Poetry."

INDEX TO FIRST LINES

PAGE

A gaunt-built woman and her son-in-law 56
A good stay-at-home season is Autumn: 106
A hundred men think I am theirs 115
A soldier, not of Fortune, but of some 141
Above me stand, worn from their ancient use, ... 191
Aloof from his tribe.......... 154
And that was when the chevaldour 139
Arch-scholar they'll call you, .. 203
Below there are white-faced throngs 140
But, Snake, you must come where we abide,............ 172
Can it be that never more..... 137
Ere Beowulf's song 105
For the poor body that I own.. 101
Foul-feathered and scald-necked,. 179
He knows Queen Lab, her isle, . 165
(He threw his crutched stick down; there came.......... 60
Here Pilate's Court is: 194
Here you should lie, ye Kings of old, ... 144
How great a front is thine—... 171
How strangely like a churchyard skull 180
I am sitting here............. 117
I am the Toy-maker; I have brought from the town...... 123
I heard in the night the pigeons.. 114
I know the answer: 'tis ingenious. 38
"I know where I'd get........ 158
I know you, Crane: 166
I think some saint of Eirinn wandering far................. 190
I'll be an otter, and I'll let you swim 157
I'm glad to lie on a sack of leaves 92

In broad daylight............. 175
In companies or lone.......... 98
In woods remote, hid in the mountain hollows,........... 201
It's my fear that my wake won't be quiet, ... 86
It was pure indeed, ... 44
"Lost," "lost," the beeves and the bullocks, ... 208
Mallo lero iss im bo nero!...... 63
Mavourneen, we'll go far away.. 113
Mould-coloured like the leaf long fallen from................. 173
My Afghan poet-friend........ 131
My eyelids red and heavy are.... 120
My wife and my comrade...... 88
My young love said to me, "My brothers won't mind, ... 109
Nor right, nor left, nor any road I see a comrade face........ 102
Not as a woman of the English.. 200
Not fingers that e'er felt...... 16
Not in a grove where each tree loses its presence, ... 145
Now comes the lad with the hazel, ... 99
O, men from the fields! 111
O what a hound he has! A hound so high................... 73
O woman, shapely as the swan, . 134
Odalisques, odalisques, ... 162
Oh, I wish the sun was bright in the sky.................... 100
Oh, to have a little house! 90
On the third day from this (Saint Brendan said).............. 47
Once I loved a maiden fair, ... 125
One day you'll come to my husband's door................ 119
Others have divers paints and enamels, ... 178
Over old walls the Laburnums.. 188
Sandalwood, you say, and in your thoughts it chimes.......... 75

PAGE

Shall I go bound and you go free, ... 108

She sat on the wall and dangled her silk-stockinged legs, ... 71

Sojourner, set down.......... 68

Stride the hill, Sower, ... 81

Sunset and silence! A man; around him earth savage, earth broken 79

That sidling creature is a little Fox: 167

The birds that soar break space . 174

"The blackbird's in the briar, .. 127

The fiddles were playing and playing, ... 110

The great ship lantern-girdled, .. 210

The Lannan Shee............. 94

The little moths are creeping... 91

The Lombards having gone back to their land, ... 192

The moon cradle's rocking and rocking 50

The Plovers fly and cry around, .. 181

The smith who made the manacles, ... 18

The stir of children with fresh dresses on, ... 121

The Swallows sang............ 4

The Thrush, the Lark, and, chief, the Nightingale, ... 153

The well—................... 3

The Wild Ass lounges, legs struck out................. 168

Then, suddenly, I was aware indeed 156

PAGE

There is an hour, they say, ... 136

There is no glory of the sunset here! 142

They have hanged Roger Casement to the tolling of a bell, .. 207

They're moaning still, ... 20

Thorough waters, thorough nations I have come.......... 209

'Tis long since, long since, since I heard.................... 104

To Meath of the pastures...... 84

"To-night," you said, "to-night, all Ireland round........... 202

Two little creatures............ 169

Up from the navel of the world, . 177

We mark the playing-time of sun and rain, ... 189

We wander now who marched before, ... 103

We watched the Condors winging towards the Moon, ... 182

We've watched the starlings flocking past the statues........ 193

When you were a lad that lacked a trade, ... 185

Where has she come from, that fawn? 74

Why do I look for fire to brand these foals? 138

With sapphire for her crown, .. 176

You had the prose of logic and of scorn, ... 205

You stay for a while beside me.. 135

You would not slumber...... 112

INDEX TO TITLES

	PAGE
Across the Door	110
An Drinaun Donn	115
Aquarium Fish	173
Arab Songs	131
Asses	158
At Cashel	191
Ave Atque Vale	209
Ballad Maker, A	125
Ballad of Downal Baun, The	50
Bat	175
Before the Fair	208
Beggar's Child, The	113
Bird of Jesus, The	44
Bird of Paradise	176
Bison	171
Blades	68
Branding the Foals	138
Breffne Caoine	200
Burial of Saint Brendan, The	47
Condors	182
Connachtman, A	86
Cradle Song, A	111
Crane	166
Crows	156
David Ap Gwillan at the Mass of the Birds	153
Dedication: To M. C. M. C.	3
Dermott Donn Macmorna	119
Drover, A	84
Dublin Roads	185
First East to West Atlantic Flyers	141
Folding Hour	99
Fuchsia Hedges in Connacht	190
Furrow and the Hearth, The	81
Garadh	101
Gilderoy	18
Girls Spinning	63
Hawaii	145
Hawaiian	75
Hornets	180
Humming-Bird	177
"I Shall Not Die for Thee"	134
Idyll, An	135
Imitation of a Welsh Poem	139
In Memory of John Butler Yeats	202
In the Carolina Woods	144
Indian	74
Interior	91
Jackdaw	154
Knitters, The	98
Laburnums	188
Landing, The	210
Legend	136
Lilac Blossoms	189
Little Fox, The	167
Man Bereaved, A	88
Men on Islands	137
Minoan	73
Miracle of the Corn, The	19
Monkeys	169
Mountaineer, A	105
Night-Fliers	174
No Child	114
Odysseus: In Memory of Arthur Griffith	205
Old College of the Irish, The, Paris	192
Old Men Complaining	60
Old Soldier	103
Old Woman of the Roads, An	90
On Two Sisters Whose Deaths Were Together	201
Otters	157
Pigeons	162
Plovers	181
Plougher, The	79
Poet, The	127
Polonius and the Ballad Singers	56
Poor Girl's Meditation, The	117
Poor Scholar of the 'Forties, A	120
Queen Gormlai	16
Rann of Exile, A	102
Reminiscence	4
Resplendent Quetzal-Bird, The	178
Roger Casement	207
Rune-Master, The	203

	PAGE		PAGE
Saint, A	121	Swift's Pastoral	38
Scanderbeg	71	Terrible Robber Men, The	100
Shall I Go Bound and You Go		Tin-Whistle Player, The	104
Free?	108	To a Poet	140
She Moved Through the Fair	109	Toy-Maker, The	123
Sister's Lullaby, The	112	Verses for Alfeo Faggi's Stations	
Snake	172	of the Cross	194
Sojourning and Wandering	106	Vultures	179
Song of Starlings	193	Wayfarer, The	142
Spinning Songs	94	What the Shuiler Said	92
Swallow	165	Wild Ass	168

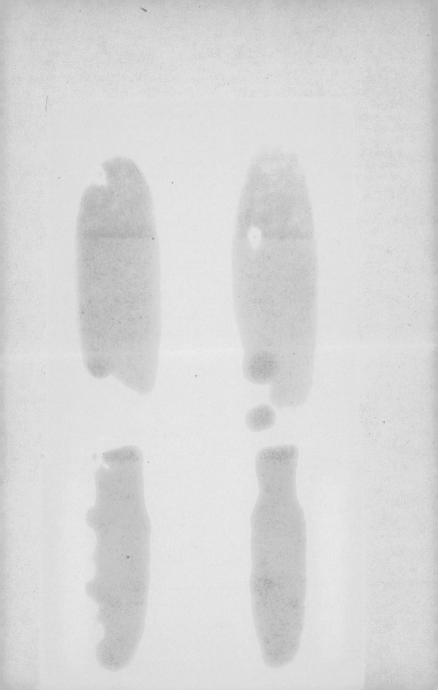

DATE DUE